Mrs. Wats

Thank you for your
constant positivity!

Look At Love Through My Eyes

Loquacious Even

Loquacious E!

DEDICATION

To the most supportive parents anyone could have –
Rev. Clinton M and the Late Mrs. Shirley B.
Thank you for teaching me how to enjoy life. I love deeply.

CONTENTS

LOOK AT LOVE THROUGH MY EYES

[iv]

ACKNOWLEDGEMENTS

SPECIAL THANKS TO

THE LORD AND SAVIOR OF MY SOUL

WHO MADE ME

BEAUTIFULLY AND WONDERFULLY IN HIS IMAGE,

PATRICE, BRANDY, JAZZ,

THOMAS, OSCAR, KENYA, KRISTAL,

ALICIA, UNFORGETTABLE TAMYE,

PARIS ANTONIO, PATTY, MALCOLM, ELAINE, AND

MY TRUE FRIENDS WHO LOVE AND

APPRECIATE ME FOR WHO I AM

LOOK AT LOVE THROUGH MY EYES

THE WORTH OF A WOMAN

Is it because I'm open to sensuality

That that is all you see?

Is it my free flowing aura that attracts your sexuality?

Or is it the way my words form to entice your senses

And start your blood flowing

That blinds all of the other aspects of me

being a woman of worth?

Yes I know what it takes to produce orgasms

of thunderous proportions

Making your toes curl, hairs stand on end,

leaving you in the fetal position

Sucking your thumb.

But in the after-glow, don't you want to know what

my synapses can effectuate?

Don't you want to hear how beautifully my mind

can connect

To things outside of the body?

[3]

LOOK AT LOVE THROUGH MY EYES

Isn't it important to you

That I can conjugate a verb and

inject imagery into descriptions

That allow you to see vividly through my eyes?

Or is it enough for you that I lay on my back or front
depending on your mood

And become, like so many before me, the pink

that you plunge into

Without feeling, emotionalism, or commitment?

Am I only worth a few minutes of sloppy

wetness and release?

Or can you see the me that lies beyond

Sexual inflections moans and groans of ecstasy?

Yes I possess the power to make your body do things

That you have only dreamed of

But my mind, heart, and soul have more to offer

Than your imagination can fathom in a nano-second.

So I ask you what is the worth of a woman?

Can her worth be measured by the number of convulsions

Created in one night?

Or can Man reach into the depths of a woman

[4]

LOOK AT LOVE THROUGH MY EYES

Seeing what God saw when He created Eve--

That she is more invaluable than any worldly possession

As well as any pinnacle of the flesh?

She is the nurturer of things living on Earth

And in the body.

She empowers from every orifice

Planting, tilling, kneading, and harvesting

ideas of the world;

Manifesting truth and love into the universe.

She is a force to be reckoned with.

So how do you measure the worth of a woman?

Just go beyond what you see

And look at the true Me.

GOOD MORNING

I see you turn over in the bed to face me. You gently kiss me then put your finger inside me with your thumb on my clitoris. You caress my neck and breast with your tongue and teeth, telling me how beautiful I am as I grind against your hand. I search for your manhood and stroke it until it awakens. Then you mount me pressing my feet against your chest forcing my knees into my chest. You enter me slowly and I feel you expanding in my walls. You tell me how much you love me and how my pussy feels so good! You feel yourself cuming but you stop and look at me. I squeeze my Kegel muscles and you laugh at the sensation. Then you scoop me up, flip me over, and elevate my legs around your waist. You put your big hand in the middle of my back forcing my face into the pillow. First you grind slowly then start beating my G from the back, spanking me and cursing that pussy while I scream in ecstasy. When you finally finish cuming, you flop on the bed next to me sweaty and sated. I jump up quickly, putting your manhood in my mouth, watching you

[6]

squirm from the sensitivity, trying to get away; but I don't stop, which

arouses you again. Then the cycle repeats.

THE MORNING AFTER

The sun came beaming in just past the half-opened blinds. I didn't want to open my eyes, but then I hear the soft, supple sound of you sleeping. I feel your even, steady breathing on my back and I realize you have wrapped your limbs around me completely. I lay there momentarily reminiscing about last night, smiling to myself. I slowly maneuver my body around to face you. You move in closer, finding comfort in my nearness and warmth. The thermal energy from your body sends sensations of delight pulsating through my senses, stirring the desire inside me again. I caress the lining of your facial structure, tracing the hair of your brows, lashes and lips with the tips of my fingers, remembering the wonderful feats you accomplished with those lips and tongue. I touch your ears, neck and head, memorizing every curvature again. I follow the muscles in your shoulder and arm with my hands, recalling how they manipulate my flesh into acrobatic positions, gently leading and transitioning me for ultimate pleasure. My fingers draw a line on your side, reaching your thighs and I pause as a tickle causes you to stir. You stretch as your senses are awakened and you open one hazel eye to see me watching you.

"Good morning," you say, continuing to stretch.

"Hello my love," is my reply.

You turn over onto your back and pull me close to lie on your chest. I revel in your closeness and soak in your aura for a moment. Then I begin again, exploring your caramel-colored playground. You moan softly as I toy with your nipples.

"You are something else," you say.

"Insatiable, incorrigible," I say as I am kissing, licking, lapping down to your happy trail.

"Yeah that!" you say marveling at the agility of my tongue.

Finally I reach my destination, gently placing you into my vocal orifice, kneading, probing, humming and slurping until you can't take any more. You push me up and with the swiftness of a cheetah; you flip and twist me onto my face. With your sword sheath, you plunge so deep inside of me I think I feel you breathing through my lungs! Gently but methodically you fill me up completely, searching for places you missed last night, hammering my G until my mind melds into a pool of euphoric bliss. I'm hoping you don't ask me to speak because my coherence is lost in the rhythm of your hips. Then my senses revitalize when comfort sets in, and I begin to meet your thrusts as I rock back into your manliness. Surprised, you let out a short burst of laughter and begin matching my intensity. Faster, deeper, harder, we go until several queefs later, we collapse from exhaustion, laughing, sweaty, and satisfied.

Then, I taste you at your most sensitive time just to see you squirm and call my name, begging me to stop. You pull me in close, cocooning me with your limbs again whispering, "Wake me up in thirty minutes." I smile to myself, pulling your face into my 44-I, and whimsically watch the clock.

BEING COMFORTABLE IN MY OWN SKIN

Can I be

Really be all of M.E.,

Mentally and emotionally

In my skin?

For deep down within

I lay out my cards to start

So there won't be any guessing.

But when an intelligent brotha

Gets wind of the true ME

They run like punks.

But why?

In my mind any man would want

An independent, intelligent woman

Who does not play games.

She knows what she wants,

And won't compromise until she gets it?

Or do they want the coy, mysterious girl

Who plays THE GAME

Toying with their manhood

Hinting at intimacy

Teasing them with small pieces of themselves

Never really satisfying the curiosities?

WHO HAS TIME FOR ALL OF THAT?!!!

Is it really that important to move

At a pace that rivals molasses in a snowstorm?

What significance does all of that have?

I have always been this way.

Is there an intellectual

That just wants a well-rounded

Individual

That knows what she wants?

I don't want to play cat and mouse.

LOOK AT LOVE THROUGH MY EYES

Why should I change my skin

To fit the normal anything?

The only beings MAN ENOUGH for the challenge

Are so young I could have breast fed them,

Or so HOOD they don't understand me.

The only thing refreshing about them

Is that they recognize

How different I am from anyone they have ever met.

Then my skin feels stretched

Trying to find some common thread

Between the lack of stimulating conversation

And the increase in sexual stamina

I'm physically ecstatic

And consciously starved,

Can I have a stallion with lust

For stimulation in every orifice?

Erotic poetry read over chocolate covered

strawberries and champagne?

Debates over the origin of religion's Genesis?

Competition for submissive positions?

Teasing texts and emails

With subtle hints of the night before?

Flashbacks of escapades

That causes my skin to quicken when I remember?

Oh, to be able to share all of M.E.

Mentally and emotionally To have this skin I'm in

Admired and loved

Without being judged and misused

Or taken out of context. I am comfortable with who I am

Why are "REAL" men so afraid?

MY STRUGGLE

Moving slowly has ALWAYS been my struggle

I know that things work out better

If you take your time

And allow things to develop

But I can't help but feel like I want to open you up

And swim in your essence

Have all of me absorbed inside of you

So I won't have to struggle with giving small pieces of

who I am to you

Resist urges to smother you with affection, attention,

and love-making

Relinquish flames of desire

That should not be exposed

According to the rules of "The Game"

Sit on my hands when you come close to me

When all I want to do is touch, tease,

[15]

LOOK AT LOVE THROUGH MY EYES

Tantalize your senses

Bite my tongue to silence the sexual rhapsodies

Flowing from my imagination to my lips

Close my mind's eye from visualizing your

warm chocolate covered skin

In the afterglow of moisture

 From a marathon of copulation

Is it more sinful for me to envision the man of God

In such a way?

First he is a man made in the image of God

Should I not yearn to be surrounded by such a man?

Will languishing always be the one emotion I feel?

BREATHE, BREATHE, BREATHE!!!

He does show his interest

Even if it is not with the intensity I wish.

Lord, work on me!

I don't want to run another man away!

[16]

LOOK AT LOVE THROUGH MY EYES

This is my struggle!

Do I give all of me?

Easily excited, loving, desirous, full of life and love

Or do I go to "The Game 101 –

How do be a player without getting played"

It's easier to just be me

I DREAMED OF YOU

I had a dream about you last night:

The room was dark at first. Then candles ignited one by one, casting a shadow of light around the room. The votives holding each light illuminated the floor, making the ambiance very seductive. Surreptitiously you approach me with the stealth of a lion stalking his prey. Once you are facing me, you don't speak. You touch my hair with your hand, stroking my locks from my hairline to the nape of my neck. You run your thumb over my lips as I gently moisten it with the tip of my tongue. You cup my face in your hands, commanding me to gaze into your eyes. You drink me in, studying all of my features. I can see the desire you have for me in your eyes. Simpatico is reflected like a mirror from my gaze. You raise my chin for a kiss, but instead you taste my lips with the tip of your tongue again and again and again. Teasing me, you begin to laugh until slowly you kiss me. You hold my lips, engulfing invisible energy from my inner power source.

Then with intensity and vigor, you spread your lips and offer

me your tongue and lips until I can hardly breathe. Longing for you

grows until it is a knot that rises to my chest, pressing on my heart,

compressing my rational thoughts, blurring the lines of reality and

fantasy. You gently release me, marveling at the hysteric euphoria

that lingers in my expression. You smile with omniscience, leading

me to a California King with eminence bed posts covered in billows of

mosquito netting. You undress me and I lay down on my back.

Lying beside me, you slowly caress my skin, memorizing every

limb and muscle. Your touch is gentle and deliberate. You watch me

to see which places generate the most pleasure. I close my eyes

enjoying the feeling of warmth from your fingers. You stroke my

thighs, running your hand closer and closer to the warmest part of

me, teasing. I open myself for your touch but you linger on my inner

thighs. You position yourself next to me so that you can lick, bite, lap,

and slurp on my left nipple and your right hand massages my clitoris

and vulva. You take some of my sweet essence and smear it on that

[19]

left nipple just to taste me. You lick your fingers then insert them

again. The way you taste my nipple I think I'll have to grow another

one! You bring me to orgasm easily. My body shakes with pleasure

and you smile at what you have accomplished.

"How do you want me to finish pleasing you?" you say.

"I want to take you for a ride," I say.

You comply by lying on your back, your rod ready for

ramming. I straddle your frame and glide your manhood easily inside

of me. I move slowly enjoying the feel of our union. I love the feel of

the shape of your head as I begin to bounce in rhythm with my hips. I

lean forward placing my hands on your chest for leverage. You close

your legs pushing your manhood deeper into my being

"Ride that shit girl!"

You always swear when it's good. I laugh, working harder,

breaking a sweat

"Wait! I don't want to cum yet!" you yell.

LOOK AT LOVE THROUGH MY EYES

I stop and we transition. You pull me onto my side and you kneel in front of me. You hold my right leg upward and enter me slowly. You place that leg on the opposite shoulder, across your body. You lean in very close to me. You press yourself all the way inside of my tunnel of love, moving ever so slowly. OMG! I did not think I could feel this close to someone! You linger, making your manhood jump inside of me. Then you begin increasing speed and intensity. I feel your veins expanding and contracting until you collapse next to me, spent.

You roll on top of me passionately kissing my lips. You move to my side, wrapping your limbs around me placing your face in my jugular and stroke my hair.

"You are so beautiful," you say, and then you fall asleep.

I awaken surrounded by toys and batteries, sweating. I could have sworn there was the faintest scent of your cologne. That's when I realize that I truly miss you

LONGING FOR LOVE

I long for a love

That stretches beyond space and time

Love that encompasses my soul

Spreading warmly through my veins

I long for a love

Full of passion, eroticism, romance

Love that does not emphasize physiology

But finds strength in my mental and spiritual being

Sensing my needs before one word is uttered

I long for a love

That looks into my face

And sees his reflection

A love that says my name

And with every enunciated syllable

I can feel his amore dripping from every letter

[22]

WHY IS LOVE SO IMPORTANT TO ME?

Why is love in a relationship so important to me??!!

Why?

I have two unprecedented parents

That show so much love and sacrifice

That it is impossible for me to want more.

I have friends that love and support me

Even accepting my faults ,

But why do I long for the love of a man

Who is anointed, passionate, romantic

With a similar sexual simpatico;

Who loves children and works in the Kingdom

Most of all he loves me

For all of my idiosyncrasies

Someone who understands what I mean

Without having to explain myself

LOOK AT LOVE THROUGH MY EYES

I see love as it manifests in marriages around me

Love that surpasses obstacles and tribulations

Love that celebrates little steps of accomplishment

Love that has its infrastructure in God

Rooted and grounded in agape

Love that knows what to say without saying it

Love that tantalizes the flesh

Seduces the mind and massages the heart

LORD HELP ME TO BE COMFORTABLE

IN MY OWN SKIN ENOUGH THAT I

DON'T HUNGER FOR SUCH A LOVE!!!

Why is it so important to me?

Then I remember I need to lay prostrate

And allow the Lover of my soul

To saturate me with His unconditional ardor

LOOK AT LOVE THROUGH MY EYES

And wait until He manifests Himself in flesh

Wait, Wait, Wait......

WHAT DOES LOVE LOOK LIKE?

What does love look like?

I Corinthians Thirteen says

"Love is not arrogant and inflated with pride

It does not insist on its own rights

Or its own way

It is not touchy, fretful, or resentful."

But what does LOVE look like?

I have seen a NEW face of love

Love turned toward me

And did not stroke my sensual desires

It peered into my face with kindness

A gentleness I have never known

Love me with sedation

Drinking in every morsel of who I am

Without touching, tasting, or teasing

My tenement

Love demonstrated unprecedented restraint

Causing me to feel for the first time

What true Godly attraction is.

Loquacious poked her head out

LOOK AT LOVE THROUGH MY EYES

To tempt fate a few times

But the NEW face of love

Would not relent to her coercion.

Strong is this strain of love

Courteous, patient, attentive

A true gentleman

Unequivocally different!

So how do I handle what love looks like now?

Never have I had to sincerely be "Eve"

When "Adam" appeared before

I maneuvered into a place where

I was in control

But now?

How do I allow myself to be truly

Subservient?

To fall into my role as help mate

Not help lead

Lord you presented this unique individual to me

So you will need to take control.

The last thing I want to do

Is kill this NEW thing

Before it has begun!

What does love look like?

I Corinthians Thirteen

"Love bears up under anything and everything that comes

It is ready to believe the best of every person

Its hopes are fadeless under all circumstances

It endures everything without weakening

LOVE – true affection for God and man,

Grows out of God's love for and in us –

It never fails!"

ON VACATION

The water is blue as the sky and the salty morning breeze flows around my face. I am wrapped in a blanket I found in the condo's closet. I always feel closer to God when I am facing the ocean. It's almost as if He is playing in the waves with His fingertips. I close my eyes and listen as the waves whisper on the shore.

The sliding glass door startles me and I jump a little. You approach me with a steaming cup of coffee.

"It's beautiful here. We should have done this sooner," you say.

I nod in agreeance. You sit directly behind me, wrapping your warmth around me. I close my eyes again, inhaling your scent mixing with the seaside air. We sit in comfortable silence for a while, enjoying our coffee and each other's nearness. You move in closer to my body from behind, removing my cup from my hands. You shuffle the blanket that was around me so that it covers us both, and you kiss me on the nape of my neck. I feel your breath on my ear,

[30]

causing my breath to quicken and my perineum muscles to quake. I lean back into your body, wishing I could melt into your being.

You begin to caress my body under the blanket making my senses come alive with arousal. You tweak my nipples with your index finger and thumb. I moan and reach behind me to rub your bald head. I can feel your desire radiating from your body. You maneuver your hands down into my pajama pants to play with my wetness while your tongue does tricks on my jugular. You slowly toy with my clitoris with your middle finger gently stroking. You make circles with your fingers and I swivel my hips to match your movements. You slide that finger inside me stirring my essence.

You remove your finger, placing it in your mouth, tasting my juices. "You taste so good early in the morning," you say.

I turn to face you as the blanket falls around us. We quickly remove our bottoms and I cover us again with the blanket. You massage your manhood, waiting for what is to happen next.

"I sure hope no one sees us," I say.

You just smile as you stroke your rod, licking your lips. You scoot down on the chaise to give me riding room. The thickness of your nine inches stands up like a flag pole. I cream again just thinking about being pleasantly filled. I hover over your body and slide your sword easily inside of my love canal. I balance myself on the palms of my feet, wrapping my arms around your neck for leverage. You bury your face into my chest sniffing my scent. I make slow up and down movements as you moan softly with a guttural groan emitting from your throat. I smile to myself enjoying your pleasure.

Surprisingly you don't rush me or take control. I continue to move methodically until my thighs begin the burn. You look up at me passionately with a bored smile. You slide down a little more, grabbing my bottom as you begin thrusting deep inside me in short bursts of excitement. I hold on to the chaise handles as you intensify your movements beneath me. I resist the urge to scream as an orgasm creeps from my toes into my thighs, back hips, canal, vulva, and lips.

The blanket begins to slip, exposing our heads. I grab it before it falls, wrapping it around my fists and the chair handles. Sweat forms on your brow as you smirk at my facial expressions. I squat closer to your body, holding the back of the chaise, positioning myself to take control so that I can get that smirk off of your face. I touch your belly as a sign for you to lie still. You brace yourself for what is coming and you wrap the blanket around your hands on the chaise. I put both of my hands on your chest, bringing my legs in closer to the chair.

I begin slowly at first, riding until I feel your manhood touch my cervix. Then with more ferocity, I increase my rhythm, arching and stretching my back, bouncing my bottom up and down. Sloppy wetness runs down your shaft and you whisper profanities into my ear. You press your face into the crook of my neck as you make that whimpering noise just before you release. I smile to myself as you sink your teeth into my shoulder to keep from calling out. I enjoy the pain and quicken my movements, coming over and over again just before you explode inside of me.

As you yell I cover your lips with a kiss to keep you from waking the neighbors. I giggle a little as you relax, shaking your head. Sitting on top of you, I wrap the blanket around our bottoms admiring your strong African features glistening from our lovemaking. I begin to trace your face when you open your eyes. You peep over your shoulder noticing an older couple drinking coffee and watching us.

You say, "Looks like we have an audience anyway." I give you a look of utter horror!

I slowly stand holding the blanket out behind me as a shield. You get up and stand in front of me, and you stroke my face before you kiss me passionately. You reach down gathering our pajama bottoms. When you stand again, you say good morning to the older couple. I shield us with the blanket as we walk back into the condo, never turning to face the couple.

"Must be mating season," the old man says, affectionately touching his wife's hand. Yep, must be," she replies with a twinkle in her eye.

AFFECTION

Cuddling, fondling, embracing, nudging, palpation

Handling, groping, perception, contingence

I long for it

I crave it

I desire it

Just one marathon of endless skin to skin, lips to lips

Fingers, nose, tongue, teeth, feet, hands

Stroking exploring needling tantalizing every sense

Not leaving one place unexplored

Beginning at the crown of my head

Slowly, slowly, slowly, slowly

Tracing my features with your metacarpals

Using your phalanges to scrutinize every crook

and crevice of my being

Lips on the nape of my neck

Fingers grasping my hair

Moving to my breasts, arms, and back

Lingering on my nipples

Whispers of naughtiness vibrating my

tympanic membrane

Spinning my mind and body

Into rapturous scenes of ecstasy

Touching me from behind

I feel the heat of your desire

Rising from your vessel

Your caressing me begins to take a toll on you

I feel the cream coming as you move to my thighs

I feel your breathing on my back

While you taste the curvature of my spine

I feel myself falling, falling, falling

Deep into a delirious, dreamy state of

ravenous pleasure

Wanting you to stop, praying that you don't

Then ever so softly you kiss me

[37]

LOOK AT LOVE THROUGH MY EYES

Penetrating me with passion I feel through my soul

Engulfing me in your arms

Squeezing me so tightly that our aortic rhythms match

Gazing into my eyes seeing your reflection

You whisper "I love you"

Knowing affection is what I needed most.

FATHER I CAN'T HEAR YOU

I am so confused

I know "the way"

And the sacrifices I must make to live "holy"

But where is my life going?

How do I crucify my flesh

So that the trap set by the enemy will not prosper?

Father, I can't hear You

Through the excitement of

Possibilities, seduction, allure, and magnetism!

Do I continue with the forward momentum of

"getting to know you"?

Or do I disregard this obvious attraction?

Do I not react to what I feel?

Father, I can't hear You!

I don't want to move into a place where You are NOT.

The safest place in the world is in Your will.

But what is Your will for my life?

Father I can't hear You

LOOK AT LOVE THROUGH MY EYES

Should I leave this one alone?

Is he sent by You?

Am I delusional?

Is my loneliness reaching out

And attracting predators of desperation?

Is the intellectual conversation

Tickling my ears

Saying what I want to hear

Stirring emotions within me

That I want to develop into a relationship

Pulling on the longing buried in the crevices of

"put this away for later"

Father I can't hear You!

I need direction and connection

Do I launch into the deep

Or continue to cope with an unfulfilled need

To be caressed passionately

Wanted for more than physical fulfillment

Intellectually stroked

Mentally stimulated

Smothered with affection

Unconditionally loved

But none of this is worth losing my place in You

Father, that's why I need to hear from You!

I can't hear You!

Blot out the things that are keeping Your voice from

speaking clearly to my being

Eradicate the distractions

That are blocking Your direct intervention

Father I can't hear You and

I refuse to move until I do!

ANXIETY

Questions questions

All in my head

Should I give my heart?

Is he great in bed?

I shouldn't think that

That's a sin.

I feel embarrassed and ashamed

What should I even think of him?

I barely know his name

I don't have a thing to lose

Life is full of many risks

I know how I feel

But through a computer screen?

What is this?

I want love in return

I have so much to give

But if I move too fast

That Loquacious gets to live

But if I move in slowly

There is apprehension even fear

Yes even at a snail's pace

The goal is to keep him near

LOOK AT LOVE THROUGH MY EYES

Keep him?

You haven't seen him

Digital images on a screen

Oh to touch him, taste him, hold him

I'm so anxious I could scream!

Now now now maybe that's it

The thing that makes men run

So much longing is thrown at him

It may end before it's begun

Ok, pull up, hold back, that's it

Heal thyself and breathe

Think only of some pleasant thought

Relax, relate, release

Think of sandy beaches, calm clear waters

Sun beaming on the sand

The wind did shift and in its trail

Was the scent of this man

Here you go again

Building your hopes

For a treacherous, ugly fall

But I can believe he could be for me

If I am to believe at all

What is there to lose?

Fear, anxiety, fantasy, driving me to write

There's more to gain

A friend a lover a soul mate for life

Fear is the problem

Been down this hopeless road before

Get all excited about a sweet young fella

Then dropped and scrapping the floor

How do I not get excited about this man?

Euphoria is the first stage

But when the chapter ends the tale

I was fired on the first page.

There has got to be someone different in him

I can feel it in my bones

I just don't want to show all my cards

And end up standing again alone

But this is how I am

This is it; this is how it is going to be

I am fearfully and wonderfully made by God

And I've got to be me

What if, what if, what if

The ultimate question at hand

But if not him

I then ask *when* will I be found by that man?

WATCHING YOU WORK

I was laying on the loveseat reading the latest installment of your master pieces. I place your book on my chest, saving my place and I begin to watch you working. Intensity blazes from your eyes, as you gaze at the laptop screen. Your lips move as you read, erase, edit, and reread your words, making certain that they flow concurrently. You moisten your lips in concentration and I shudder as I remember this morning's adventure:

You awaken me with kisses on the center of my back. Your large, masculine hands are stroking my skin and hair. You move your hips close to mine and I can feel your "Good Morning" erection poking me into complete alertness. You fondle my left nipple with your left hand, gently maneuvering me onto my back. You roll on top of me nuzzling my neck with your nose, tickling my jugular with your tongue.

"Good morning queen," you say. As I giggle at the sensation I say, "Good morning sweet king."

[45]

LOOK AT LOVE THROUGH MY EYES

I moan softly as I reminisce and close my eyes trying to resist the urge to touch myself. It startles you. In all of your concentrating you forgot I was there. You glance up from your fixed stare a little annoyed. You notice that my eyes are closed and an omniscient smile crosses your face. Knowing what is on my mind you remove your glasses and cross the room to join me on the loveseat. You lean in gently kissing and teasing me. Reaching down between my legs, you expertly remove my panties with one hand. With your forefinger and thumb, you massage my clitoris continuing to kiss my lips. You place your fingers inside of me, stirring the juice. You withdraw the fingers, placing them in your mouth as if you are teasing an entrée you have been preparing. You turn my body so that my legs are dangling off of the loveseat and you sit on the floor with your legs crossed in front of me.

You position my legs to rest on your shoulders, pulling my bottom half closer to your mouth. You tease my clitoris with your tongue, flickering and licking ever so slowly. Then with sudden voracity, you devour me with a renewed appetite. I try to pull away from you, but you wrap your arms around my legs placing your hands firmly on my thighs. Restricted from moving, I scream and my face is covered in total ecstasy, not expecting to have any flesh left when you finish. OH MY GOODNESS!! WHERE DID YOU LEARN TO DO THAT THING WITH YOUR TONGUE?!! Orgasm comes quicker than I anticipate, leaving you covered in my essence. You drink me in as if I were a Big Gulp, leaving love's juices surrounding your goatee.

Without removing my legs from your shoulders, you slowly rise to your feet gliding my body back to the cushions. You enter me easily because of the self-lubrication you induced. With slow, steady thrusts you revel in my wetness, trying to control your ejaculation.

"If God made anything better, he kept it for Himself," you say.

I giggle, enjoying the feel of your manhood filling me up from lips to hips. You spread my legs eagle-like to watch your shaft glisten with my oil, as you continue to move with pain-staking slowness. You transition to straddle one of my legs leaving the other on your

[47]

shoulder to get in closer and deeper. I can feel the head of your

manliness tapping the edge of my cervix and feel my belly jumping. I

can almost taste what you had for dinner last night! Finally, your

steady movements quicken. Like a roaring lion you release, vibrating

the china into a symphonic hum. You collapse on top of me, smiling.

"You are a wonderful distraction, but I must get some work

done," you say.

You rise pulling me with you to shower. Then I am dry,

refreshed, and laying on the loveseat again; You, back at the computer

screen, but this time you are whistling. I pick up your current master

piece and resume my position – watching you work.

IS IT TRUE?

I have your attention

Vocabulary mixed with sensual pleasure

Words mingled with desire

But are you for real?

I hear your verbalizing intensity

Saying the right things

Me wanting to believe the sincerity I sense

in your inflections

Discerning your passion and wittiness

I can picture you gazing into the looking glass

Seeing the reflection of my beautiful aura

Covering you with my ambience

Affecting your senses

Changing your perspective of life, love,

and happiness

But is it true?

Do you mean it when you say

This relationship can develop without one taste

of your manhood?

LOOK AT LOVE THROUGH MY EYES

Without one touch of your masculinity igniting my virility?

Soft vitality longing for the strokes of manliness?

Instead you offer intellectual prowess

To mentally weaken my fortitude

You offer erotic interludes coated with verbal cunning

Creating imagery consisting of rose petals

and chocolate covered strawberries

And caramel delight

But is it true?

Are you a reality?

So much of me wants to believe

Something inside of me is scratching at the wall built by

Disappointment, hurt, and rejection

I want to believe all that you say!

But is it true?

Are you really who you say you are?

Continue to stroke my intellect

Tantalize my sensibilities

And allow Cronos to prove to me

You are unmistakably true.

SCHOOL GIRL

Why does the slightest attention from a man

Send me into a tailspin?

I am beautifully and wonderfully made in His image

I should take compliments with grace and decorum

But instead I become a 14 year old virgin

Giddy and nervous

Excited all day

Unable to sleep nights

Anticipating the next encounter

By phone, email or IM

Heaven forbid we meet!

If I am allowed to drink in his aura

Envelop his personality

Swim in his intellect

Try his anointing with mine

Watch him undress me with his eyes

Tease him with my wittiness

Why does the slightest attention from a man

Send me into a tailspin?

Awakening that longing deep within me

To engulf a masculine being

Embracing him completely

Mind, body, soul, and spirit

Being the woman God called me to be

For the man He ordained for me to be with

Why does the slightest attention from a man

Send me into a tailspin?

Because I long for unconditional love

SOMEONE NEW

I want to be open enough

To receive all that you have to offer

To make love to your entire being

Until even your soul is like

A molten ball of euphoric flesh

Mixing every flavor of you

Savoring your essence

Leaving an aroma akin to worship

Even creation pays attention

FEAR – false evidence appearing real

I recite it over and over

Mentally feeling my past hurt

Disappointment, mistrust

Stabbing at my present

Longing for your touch

LOOK AT LOVE THROUGH MY EYES

Craving your kisses

Pushing the idea of your masculinity

Wrapped around my docility

Back into Pandora's Box

"Don't think that! Don't be in a hurry!"

The Rules of Love twist and turn in my head!

Repeat Replay Rephrase Restate

Why is love always a GAME?

Why can't I just be who I am?

Eager to love

Eager to please

Venereal, erotic, funny, passionate

Easily read, easily attached

Easy to love, spoiled to the core

Maybe I'm just in love with the idea of being in love?

NEVER ENOUGH TIME

My phone rings and I know it's you by the ringtone.

"Hello my love." I say.

"Hello mamacita. I am on my way home. They cancelled night work," you say.

"I'm on my way!" I rely.

"See you in a few." You disconnect.

I hang up and rush to my car, praying I don't get a ticket, trying to get to your apartment. We have got to do something about the two of us living on opposite ends of the city! I reminisce about our first encounter. All of the reservations you had before you let me taste you. All of the apprehension, doubts, and fears you had bottled up inside of you were killing your soul. With one carefully planned bout of spontaneity, you admitted to feeling like the dead had arisen. I'm glad because I was beginning to think that you didn't have a pulse. We talked earlier and you recalled how wet I was once you entered me. I recalled how you placed your hands under my hips, tilting my cervix upward for deeper penetration. The memory makes the perineum muscles in my vagina jump and I press on the accelerator to get to you.

As I pull into your complex, I call you to tell you that I'm here. I park and pull a small bag from the back seat. I sprint up the stairs and knock on your door. You open it wrapped in a towel and take a couple steps back allowing me to enter. As I close the door, we don't even speak. You pull me close to you, grabbing the back of my head, passionately kissing me. It's so intense I think I can feel heat rising from your skin. I rip the towel from around your waist and push you onto the couch. I place your manhood into my mouth savagely, as if I hadn't eaten in days. I move to slurp, lick, and hum on your testicles and you scream, "Oh shit!" Your body begins to rise from the couch from the fervor of my foreplay. I wrap my arms around your legs with my palms on your torso pressing your body back down onto the couch.

"What….are…you…trying…to…do…to do...to….me...girl?"

I giggle and continue. After a few more insistent moans, I rise quickly throwing my clothes everywhere. I place a packaged condom between my teeth. I rip open the package then carefully place it on your erection with my mouth.

You watch in amazement. "Oh you gone get it tonight little lady."

You jump on top of the couch straddling my body. You gently glide your manhood deep inside of me, savoring my wetness.

"Damn your pussy is wet just like I like it."

You start slowly then you increase speed and duration with short bursts of roughness. I feel a sting on my left butt cheek. When I look back, I see a small leather paddle in your hand.

"Ride it like you stole it Daddy!" I say.

"Yee-haw!" you say.

[57]

We both laugh until you spank me again. I erupt with an orgasm and you continue the rodeo match. You jump up and pull me to dining room table. You clear the table with one swoop of your hand. You throw me on top of the table, pulling my hips to the edge. You place one leg on each shoulder, entering me with a new urgency. Our bodies are so close together, I can bend my knees over your back. With quick short strokes, you give it to me and I cum over and over again. I feel like my chest is going to collapse if I have another orgasm.

You continue to hammer my G, making swivel motions with your hips. Your rhythm changes and your strokes get longer and shorter.

"I'm not ready to release yet," you say.

You pull out and sit in one of the dining room chairs without arms. I straddle your erection, using the chair back and the floor for leverage. I grind slowly and methodically, relishing our oneness. I see the sheer pleasure of our lovemaking all over your face. Passion makes your eyes look like little slits in your expression.

"Ride that dick baby," you say.

I smile and turn around into reverses cow girl. I hold on to the table and bounce and bounce and bounce. In mid-bounce you carry me to the couch again. The top half of my body is hung over the top of the couch. You swiftly enter me from the back with renewed zeal, until you roar like a lion in an unbelievably loud climax. You pull out and stretch out beneath my legs on the couch, sweaty and satisfied. I'm still hanging over the couch, heady from the amusement park ride I've just experienced. Somewhere in the other room we both hear that Nextel clicking. Some contractor is demanding your attention once again. When I love the hardest working man alive, there is never enough time.

YOU'VE GOT MY MIND REELING!

You've got my mind reeling!

From the very first day we talked

I'm trying to keep my focus

But when you say my name

I can't help but get caught

I'm trying to keep my balance

Keep my flesh under control

But every time you open your mind

And allow creativity to drip from your lips

I find myself falling, falling, falling

Into your deep passionate intonations

Swimming in the ecstasy of your thoughts

Basking in the afterglow of your eloquence

How easily you express inventiveness

From one suggestion from my mind

You take my thought and taste my declarations,

Digesting every syllable

Then you turn to me reflecting all of my conjecture

Matching my animation, eroticism, and strength

You are not intimidated by my intelligence

LOOK AT LOVE THROUGH MY EYES

Returning every emotion felt with equal amounts of

stamina and voracity

Never have I experienced such intensity

Mental acceleration cocooned in passionate avidity

You've got my mind reeling!

I go through my daily routines

Teaching, talking, laughing, sharing

But thoughts of you reoccur

Replay, repeat, recap, rephrase, replay

Thoughts of role playing, romanticism

Hoping, wishing, praying, everything you say is real

Imagining our first physical encounter

Physical not in the sense of sexuality,

 but intimate rendezvous

Mingled with savvy conversation

Immersed with intellectual wittiness

Intuitiveness like never before

You've got my mind reeling!

I have heard of meeting someone that reflects who you are

I have prayed for someone to be that for me

But to gaze into your reflection and actually see myself in you

LOOK AT LOVE THROUGH MY EYES

Will be indescribable, incommunicable

I can almost feel your aura surrounding my being

Stretching through time and space

Wrapping your entire subsistence around who I am

You've got my mind reeling!

Soul mate, confidant, consort, companion?

I know what I feel…

Bewilderment, befuddled, flabbergasted, dumbstruck,

Mystified, perplexed, rattled, shocked, disoriented

I'll know for sure when I touch you!

Taste, caress, explore, encourage

Umm to just drink you in!

To finally look into your eyes

Watch that all knowing snicker spread across your face

Seeing my name flow from your succulent lips…

The anticipation is DEADLY!!

You have truly got my mind reeling!

I MET A KING

I adore beginnings

The euphoria of emotion

The discovery of sensations

Redefined by a new exploration of flesh

Mentally tantalizing the inside of the soul

Developing fresh feelings of infatuation

Stirring questions of "what if"

I can still hear your voice

Intellectual inflections

Stimulating my sensibilities

Pulling my mind into a state of flux

Bubbling excitement

Filling every orifice

Until I can hardly breathe

I can still feel your thumb

Gently touching the nape of my neck

I reminisce about our extensive conversation

Four hours of verbal intercourse

You left my mind reeling

The essence of your quirkiness

Swimming in my cerebral cortex

LOOK AT LOVE THROUGH MY EYES

Your eyes blazing chestnut

As my personality is mirrored in your aura

You reflecting my assertiveness

That could only be sensed through a touch

And to my surprise mid-sentence

You kissed me

Softly, cautiously

Our first intimate encounter

What did you say when I asked why?

"It just felt right."

I agree ☺

I replay the desire that shines in your eyes

When you look at me

Thinking naughty thoughts

I can feel longing rising from my toe nails

Surging to my vulva

Pulsating through every blood vessel

I close my eyes to try to suppress the need

To rip your clothes off

And devour you inch by inch

Piece by piece

Until we are not reflections of one another

LOOK AT LOVE THROUGH MY EYES

But one complete entity

Covered in God's anointing

Intertwined with passion, romance, and eroticism

Filling every void

I remember your embrace

How you consumed me in your presence

Your kisses touching my inner core

Probing, nibbling little pieces of me

Masculinity igniting femininity

I remember the feel of your manliness

Teasing me from behind clothing

Your hands on my 44 I

Your large palm on my back

Curiosity surging through me

Then the release

You gaze into my mirror

Seeing your wanting reflected in my face

Me not wanting to leave your presence

You wishing I could stay longer

Both of us lamenting over our meeting

Mingling with "Family"

Glancing at each other

LOOK AT LOVE THROUGH MY EYES

Wanting to retreat to that quiet place again

Then we part

And I wonder what will happen next?

I anticipate greatness…

True Blue

I WANT YOU

You amaze me.

It never fails

Every time we talk

You astonish me with your thoughts

So long have I longed for an indescribable,

inexpressible, unexplainable…

OH OH OH!!! I can't make the feeling audible!

I want you!

Not just the physical satisfaction of your

masculinity enfolded around my body

As if it was destined to be so from the beginning of time,

But to feel the God in you ignited inside of me

The way Eve was originated specifically for Adam

Using his own flesh and blood.

To experience the inoculation of your love

Weeding out the hurt and disappointment of the past

To taste the empiricism of love written by Solomon

LOOK AT LOVE THROUGH MY EYES

From the one who captured his heart.

"Let him kiss me with the kisses of his mouth!

For your love is better than wine."

(Songs of Solomon 1:2)

"You have ravished my heart and given me

courage with one look from your eyes."

(Songs of Solomon 4:9)

I want you!

To revel in your quirkiness

Swim in your intelligence

Glean from your learn-ed book sense

Debate your ineludible opinion on matters

Bathe in your eloquence

I want you!

I can't help but wonder

What can I do to position myself to be found by you?

Found loving, laughing, caring, nurturing,

and uniting with all of who you are

LOOK AT LOVE THROUGH MY EYES

Found by you not as an acquaintance or buddy

With stimulating conversation

in the wee hours of the night

But a helpmate, confidant, homie-lover-friend for life.

I want you! The ultimate question is how long will it be

before you want me?

SECURITY INTERRUPTED

The snow was falling slowly, covering the ground in big flakes adding to the accumulation from the day before. Through the window, I could just see it falling over the rise and fall of your shoulder. The sheets were wildly askew but the heat from our bodies and love-making clung to the air. My weekend getaways to New York have always been spectacular, and this weekend was no exception.

As we bask in the after-glow and I listen to you breathe, a violent knock at the door startles us. You bolt up grabbing your gun, heading for the door buck naked. I jump up and throw on my pajamas, as you peak through the blinds.

"Hold on!" you yell through the door.

I toss you some pants and you open the door as you slide them on."I'm sorry to disturb you, Captain, but we have an incident that requires your attention." The man glances at my face, noticing my displeasure.

You say, "Okay, give me a minute." You rush past me into the bedroom, throwing things around getting dressed. You toss your cuffs on the bed, sitting down to put on your shoes.

"I'm sorry babe, duty calls."

I fondle the cuffs remembering last night. "Ummmhummm…" I say.

"You okay with this?" you ask, eyebrow raised.

I say, "If I say no, will you stay with me? It's my last day here."

You turn back, continuing to get dressed. I open the handcuffs and walk to block the door. You scramble around talking to yourself, making a mental list, checking for everything you need.

LOOK AT LOVE THROUGH MY EYES

"Handcuffs….," you say then look up at me. As you walk

toward me, you add, "I'm really sorry about this, babe. I promise not

to be long."

As you lean to kiss me, I cuff our wrists together.

You look up with fury in your eyes. "Did you just cuff me?"

you whisper with rage.

Your officer is still standing in the door way. "Okay, Captain,

I'll call you later to debrief." Your man was gone. You grab our

wrists and flip me onto the bed. You pounce on top of me like a lion

devouring its prey. You pin down my wrist that is connected to yours.

You stare down at me with a mixture of excitement, anger, and desire

in your eyes, making them glow.

"You are going to suffer the consequences for

this spoiled rotten behavior," you say.

I'm speechless, excited, and aroused all at the same time.

You lean down licking my jugular causing

72

me to shiver really hard.

"Don't be afraid now you started this."

I chuckle nervously, unable to speak. You slowly remove your pants and gun belt with the one free hand and then you work on my pajama pants. I look down at your manhood and it is fully extended, thick, and throbbing. My mouth begins to water.

You notice and command, "Don't touch it! You do as I say."

A smile threatens my face but I quickly extinguish it. You pull us up into the riding position. You reach into the night stand and pull out a leather skull Spank-HER. You look at me and command, "RIDE!"

I position myself froggie style over your big ass body and glide your manhood into my sloppy wetness. I slowly bob up and down, leaning on your chest with both hands. The anger in your eyes ebbs as you feel my juices running down your shaft. I close my eyes and I am enjoying the sensation of you thickening within my walls, when I get a sharp sting on my left butt cheek.

You smirk. "Ride, I say ride!"

I lean in closer to your body pushing up for leverage and ride your dick like a stolen vehicle. You curse and call on the Most High, swinging the spank-HER in intermittent spurts.

"Stop! Stop! I don't want to cum yet!" you say. Thankfully, I transition, feeling the burn in my thighs. You pull me to the edge of the bed, pinning my handcuffed arm behind my back. My face is in the covers. I hear a buzzing noise and I realize you don't plan to hit it from the back. You uncuff your arm and cuff me behind my back while I'm in doggie style position. I hear you pull up a chair and sit behind me.

"So you don't want your man to go to work, hummmm?"

You insert the Jack Rabbit inside me and begin to slowly torture me.

"No Daddy, I know you have to work."

The Rabbit amps up a notch. I moan in ecstasy.

"So why didn't you just let me go this time?"

The Rabbit moves in rapid motion.

"My time is limited and I want all of you while I'm here," I say.

"Hummmm," you say, as you speed the Rabbit up to high on all levels. I scream as I cum over and over again!

You slowly remove the toy and devour me from behind as if I were a full course meal. I squirm to get away but you intertwine your arms around my legs, pulling me closer to the edge of the bed. I feel like an erupting volcano of never ending lava, listening to you slurp and moan as I cum and squirt and cum and squirt and cum and squirt. Air pressure compresses in my lungs as I struggle to breathe, tears blur my vision. I see circles, moons, and stars. I lose all senses. Then you stand bulging and erect, hard enough to cut glass.

LOOK AT LOVE THROUGH MY EYES

You plunge into my wetness forcefully, hitting bottom in short bursts, making me cry out. You lean in, releasing my restraints, kissing, and nipping my back. You pull my legs up around your waist and pound my G slowly at first. Then you move with more vivaciousness. You roar like Tarzan as your essence warms my insides, touching my soul.

You flip me over; lay on top of me, passionately kissing. You pour your love inside my being with every flick of your tongue.

"You gone have to learn how to behave, little lady. I can't keep missing work." All I can muster is a smile as I caress your head and you undress us both. As you gather me into your arms, I hazily watch the snow fall through the window.

I IMAGINE

I imagine in my mind

Scenes of you and me

Holding, touching, kissing, caressing

Trying desperately to devour each other

Tasting desires sweet juices

So much so

Until I can't catch my breath

Feeling your large sun-kissed hands

Surrounding my face

Watching you drink me in through your eyes

Seeing wonder and amazement

Twinkling in your stare

Gazing into the lasciviousness

That I feel creeping from your loins

Watching it spread to all of your limbs

Scalding me through your fingertips

Longing so intense

That I'm sure we'll burn a hole in the universe

Then you slowly caress my hair

As you utter praise and worship from your lips

LOOK AT LOVE THROUGH MY EYES

Giving honor to the Most High

For lending you His gift

And ever so gently you pull me close to you

As our lips touch

Anointing ignites, binding our souls into one entity

Merging spirituality, physiology, sexuality, and eroticism

Into a ministry destined from the beginning of time

I imagine you taking me into your arms

Shielding me from the trauma of change

Reminding me like God

That you promised to never leave me

I imagine endless days of

Laughter, passion, and romance

Long sleepless nights of love making

Playful mornings before coffee

I imagine you cocooning your love around me

Pressing my essence so deeply into your being

That I see you in me

I imagine us having pillow talk

Even when we are standing in a crowd

LOOK AT LOVE THROUGH MY EYES

Watching people watching us
Marveling at what God has done
I see me singing love songs to you
And you greedily taking all of me
Tasting every note
Savoring every melody

I imagine where we will be
When you realize that you love me
What we are doing when you use those three little words
Dripping with agape

I pray that my images have not just been a cruel dream
But I must thank God for my vivid imagination.

LOOK AT LOVE THROUGH MY EYES

I TOUCH MYSELF

I touch myself

And I feel your hands

Touching my clitoris

I feel your fingers massaging me into climax

Then your tongue

Lapping my warm essence

I touch my breast

And I feel your hands, juicy lips and tongue

Biting, tasting, touching, slurping

Every inch of my nipples

I touch myself

And I feel your hands

Examining every limb and muscle

Awakening every nerve ending

From "my hair follicle to my toe nails." (Thanks Jill)

I touch myself

LOOK AT LOVE THROUGH MY EYES

And I feel your hands

Stroking my hair

Your succulent lips and tongue

Nuzzling my neck and ears

Ever so slightly

Teeth teasing my jugular

Nose inspiring my scent

Words of ardor, passion, desire, admiration

Expiring from your lips

I touch myself

And I feel your hands

Caressing my face

Your lips kissing my cheeks, chin, eyes – my lips

Me tasting the worth of your love

I touch myself

And I feel your hands

Guiding your manliness to the right orifice

Teasing my clitoris with the head of your desire

LOOK AT LOVE THROUGH MY EYES

Then you find the core me

And slowly thrust your manhood

Into my body, soul, and spirit

Planting your seeds of life, love and longing

Solidifying our union

Me incubating and nurturing

You and I

I touch myself

And I feel your hands

Pulling me close to bask in after glow

Feeling your moist skin

As you wrap your limbs around me, comforting me

Assuring me that this is not all that you wanted

Bathing me in your mantle

Until you return for more of the first

I touch myself

And I feel you

I COULD LOVE HIM

I could love him

I really could you know

His prodigious smile

His incorrigible laughter

His thirst for knowledge and truth

I could love him

I drank him in last night

Not like a big gulp on a 100 degree day

More like a tall glass of VSOP

That warms the body inside and out

Leaving little beads of sweat on your upper lip

I inhaled the essence of who he is

At first he is tropical sunshine in 70 degree weather

Fresh, breezy waves of crisp air

Refreshing to the senses

By midnight he was a warm masculine cocoon

LOOK AT LOVE THROUGH MY EYES

Encasing my thoughts

Teasing and toying with passion

Exuding lust like a stallion

Longing to win the race

I had to touch him

I couldn't help it

I wanted to feel his exuberance

Tantalize his core

Stroke his potential

I love the way he looks at me

Like he could tear me apart

And slowly put me back together again

I love the look of admiration

After a coy "teaching moment"

How he sponges the knowledge

Storing it for later use

He teases me

LOOK AT LOVE THROUGH MY EYES

Knowing I hate "No"

Feeling for undetermined boundaries

Touching crevices of my femininity

That have not been stimulated in a while

The beginning is always the best

Keeping it fresh is the hidden key to success

Do I risk it?

Loving and not receiving love in return

Can I be satisfied with half of him?

Never touching, tasting, melding into

All of who he is

Risking the loss of self

To enjoy feeling desirable again

I could love him completely

THE RENDEVOUS

We have been planning this trip for months, and now the time has come. I check and recheck my bags for this weekend. One bag has lingerie that was surreptitiously chosen by you. They are surrounded by an assortment of toys, potions, and props to feed my imagination. I smile at the possibilities. I finish packing and dress carefully.

You mentioned that your favorite piece of lingerie is the pink satin. I dress in the pink satin bustier and struggle to make sure the seam is straight on the panty hose. I think to myself, "He won't see this coming." I put on my silk blouse and pencil skirt. In my carry-on bag I place my black pointed toed 4 ½ inch stilettos. You love big legs in heels! On my feet are sensible shoes that I'll change once I land in Baltimore.

When the cab comes, I check the house alarm and make sure everything has been turned off. The driver takes my bags and we head for the Charlotte Douglas International Airport. I can still hear

your voice from our conversation last night. Your excitement was

contagious. You told me that you had several surprises for me, but one

in particular would change our lives forever. I still wonder what it is.

Like most women, I dream of marriage and children, but I would hate

to assume anything. Because you live in Atlanta, which is not too far

from Charlotte, the distance between us could have been a major

issue; however, I am proud of what we have accomplished together.

I arrive at the airport and move to stand in the long line for

security. I wind my way around with shoes on, shoes off. I trot to

Starbuck's for a Java Chip with an extra shot. I'm too nervous to eat.

As I sit down at the gate, my phone rings.

"Hello."

"Hey princess, are you at the airport?

"Yes, my sweet prince. I am ready to see you."

"What are you wearing?"

"Red silk and my sexiness."

"I'm sure you are. Well I'll see you in a few."

"I can't wait!" We disconnect.

As soon as I hang up the flight attendant calls my row to board. Your friends at the airline are very hospitable. I did not anticipate a first class ticket, which is a first for me. I really am a princess today! As I sit down, the flight attendant hands me a brochure detailing the Fell's Point Dinner Experience and a small box. Surprised, I open my new box. Inside are a card and a wrist corsage made of Hybrid Tea Gemini roses. The card reads, "Love is not finding the right person, but creating a right relationship. It's not about how much love you have in the beginning but how much love you build till the end. (Source Unknown) I am anticipating greatness for us, my Queen."

Oh my goodness! You are truly doing it up this weekend! I put on the corsage and leaf through the pamphlet that was given to me. After a snack and a tasty glass of Asti, I relax and watch God's wonders floating past the window in the sky. All I can think about is how I'm going to put it on you tonight.

LOOK AT LOVE THROUGH MY EYES

As the plane lands, I collect my things and head for the luggage turnstile. According to my itinerary, my flight arrives twenty minutes before yours. I wait patiently in the airport for you to arrive. I watch the people walking, meeting, and embracing. I anticipate what you will do when we finally see each other, finally alone without distractions of any kind. My mind recalls all of the mental foreplay we have experienced over the last few months. You stroking my intellect with words of ardor, passion, and romanticism. Me caressing your ego with words of pride, admiration, and strength. Now after arranging and rearranging schedules, we are going to be together. The anxiety I feel cannot be explained. It is akin to the feeling I got as a teenager right before I had sex for the first time. My stomach is in knots, my throat is dry, and my hands are sweaty. Oh my goodness! The anticipation is killing me! Breathe girl breathe!

My cell phone buzzes. The text says, "I've landed! The plane is on da runway. R u ready 4 me?"

I smile to myself and reply, "Come and see! LOL I'm n da luggage area waitn."

NOW I'M REALLY NERVOUS! I run to the restroom to potty for the fourth time. I look at myself in the mirror again, checking my hair, makeup, and clothing for the hundredth time. I change my shoes and check my pantyhose seams. Relax, breathe and enjoy I say to myself. After touching up my lipstick again, I wheel my stuff out and search the crowd for you.

The terminal traffic has multiplied by about 300 people. I move toward the turnstile where your flight is listed. I stand in the center of the crowd surveying the area. I feel your hands on my waist before I hear your voice.

"You are more beautiful than I remembered."

I feel your lips brushing my ear and I am instantly inundated by your nearness. I close my eyes losing touch with all reality for a moment. You gently turn me around to face you. I reach up touching your clean shaven head as you bow a little, enjoying my touch. You gaze into my eyes and we both smile. Like an invisible magnet drawing kinetic energy toward its original source, we connect in a slow kiss, drinking in each other's aura. We disconnect, collecting

ourselves and begin searching for cab.

"Where are we going?" I ask.

"Will you allow me to surprise you?"

"By all means. But trust I will not be the only one surprised this

weekend."

You laugh gleefully, leading me to the awaiting transportation.

We ride, discussing the history of the place you have chosen. We

come to our destination facing the Baltimore Harbor. We approach

the Admiral Fell Inn and I am completely giddy. The bellman takes

us directly to the Yellow Room. I almost collapse when I enter the

suite, marveling at the vaulted ceilings and the California King

strategically placed in the center of the room. The separate sitting

area stirs my inventiveness, causing my imagination to go into a

serious upswing. The bellman places our bags down as you sneakily

watch my reaction to the room.

Once again you are behind me, this time kissing the nape of my

neck. You gently slide my skirt zipper down, causing it to fall to the floor. You reach your arms underneath mine expertly unbuttoning my blouse from behind. I am amazed at the agility of your fingers on the tiny buttons. Once my blouse falls to the floor, you are surprised to see the ensemble that I have strategically placed beneath my clothing. I slowly spin around to face you. My body is outfitted in the soft pink satin bustier, with the matching thong and garter. You even notice the old school pantyhose with the seam down the back of my full-figured thighs and calves. You bellow with excitement once you realize what you see.

"You are full of surprises huh?!"

I'm cheesing at your enthusiasm. You rush to get undressed, but I stop you.

"Wait! My surprise is not complete! Sit here on the edge of the bed and be patient. I'll be back," I say.

I reach for my bag, removing a CD. I ask you to find the CD player and I get a chair from the sitting room. I position myself in the chair directly in front of the bed. You stretch out with your head at the foot of the bed, wearing only your boxers. You are watching me intently. I give you a furtive smile using my "Rock the wrestler's" eyebrow. I silently pray that my B-Risqué classes pay off right now.

You press play on the CD player in expectancy of what is about to happen. Toni Braxton's "Breathe" comes on and I begin to move in rhythm, trying to remember the routine. I sway seductively, bending, stretching, and extending my limbs, hips, and torso. When I lean back   and spread my legs to their fullest length, you notice that my thong is crotchless. You jump on top of the bed, bouncing up and down like you are three years old. I start laughing so hard I just stop dancing and fall out of the chair onto the floor. We both laugh until we have tears in our eyes. When I look up, you are standing over me naked and fully erect.

You extend your hand to help me up. You lead me to the bed and gently remove my corset, garter, thong, and pantyhose. The desire in your eyes could burn a hole through the earth. As I lay on my back you start at my toes, massaging and tasting, moving up my right leg. As you taste my right knee, I can feel your fingers exploring my clitoris and stirring my juices. You position yourself between my

93

thighs and guide my left leg into the air. You position yourself across my body, yet you are facing me holding my left leg. You enter me gently, contouring your body to the curve you've made with my legs. You balance yourself on your left arm lifting your right leg and hips, angling your manhood downward into my body. Slowly you gyrate, savoring my wetness.

I look into your masculine features, basking in our closeness; secretly wishing it would never end. You take my left leg and turn my body onto my right side. You lift my left leg and enter from behind. You move more quickly keeping a steady rhythm. I must not be making enough noise for you, because you pound your manhood into me in intermittent bursts.

"Oh yes Daddy! Give it to me!" I scream.

We shift again and I find myself standing with my face buried in the covers of the California King. I feel something cold and slimy, and then you massage my anal cavity until I barely feel your fingers.

"Relax baby. I promise to move slowly," you say.

LOOK AT LOVE THROUGH MY EYES

I feel you licking and lapping on my spine. You caress my clitoris with your fingers, entering in and out. I feel you slowly pressing your rod into my anal cavity. Pain shoots through me like shocks of electricity. You don't rush or push until you feel me relax again. Patiently, you inch your rod into me until I can feel your head on my G-spot. Once you touch my G, you notice my reaction. With slow, gentle thrusts you tap my core until you feel me relax completely. You make your movements more deliberate and steady.

To your surprise I whisper, "Spank me baby," and then it is on! You increase ferocity. And I feel an orgasm like never before creeping   up from my toes, sending an indescribable, intangible potency through every limb, muscle, artery, vein, cell, neutron, electron, and nucleus,   until I think I will surely be the first case of sexual combustion! The explosion comes suddenly and we sound like Tarzan and Jane in an urban jungle swinging from tree to tree.

We succumb to ecstasy and fatigue at the same time, you lying on my back across the bed. My mind is flustered trying to grab hold of what just happened. You roll onto the bed glistening from lovemaking. Your eyes are closed and I'm watching you, smiling. You open one eye, sensing my gaze. You gather me into your arms holding me, playing in my hair, and caressing my face. I wallow in your aura, forgetting about space and time, never wanting to leave this moment.

Then I hear the even steadiness of your breathing. You are sleeping cocooned around me. I free one arm and touch your face, tracing your features. Just above your head I see a piece of paper poking out from underneath the pillow case. When I pull the paper free from its hiding place, I discover a deed for a house you purchased in my neighborhood.

LOVE FROM A STORM

I found love in a the midst of a storm

Wandering aimlessly

Reaching for something that resembles hope

Drawing from the sorrow of loss

Swimming in self-pity and loneliness

Wrestling the winds of bitterness

Pushing at the thought that I was meant to live like Paul instead of Ester

When out of nowhere love appeared

First as a few kind words

Developing into conversation

Then long sleepless nights of passionate ear-phonic melodies

Then one night

I saw love

Experienced what it feels like to touch agape

My anointing jumped within me

Destiny tickled my ears with scripture

I could feel for the first time

LOOK AT LOVE THROUGH MY EYES

What a soul tie is

An all encompassing magnetism

That enveloped every part of me at "Hello"

To hear love say "You're worth it"

And know it's not a line

To listen to love speak of God

To feel God's presence

When love enters the room

Then the winds of the storm shift again

But this time love covers me with its protection

Because protector is love's name

Covering the harsh words of criticism

Shielding me from life's negativity

Reminding me that love is patient, kind,

long suffering and mine.

Then I feel love's parasol

From the wind, rain, lightening, thunder

Ushering me into the peace of God

As only love can

Because love found me and made me his own

YOU

All my life I've waited

Waited for the one

The one who would love, care, protect

Enjoy, embrace, and indulge in

The essence of me.

Now you're here

What do I do?

I want you to know

Every nook and cranny of

L-O-Q-U-A-C-I-O-U-S

What moves me, stirs me

Makes me laugh and cry

What causes my juices to flow

Turning me inside out and back again

I'm scared because I love you

With every beat of my heart

Every surge of life pulsating through my veins

God knows I love you

But I can't help being pulled…

Pulled to give more

Pulled to hold back

LOOK AT LOVE THROUGH MY EYES

Pulled to smother you

With sum and substance

Allowing you to glimpse

The soul fire deep within my existence

The innermost places only God has seen

Pulled to extinguish the desire of such exposure

Which ignites fear that you'll run away

To know you

The You of you

The you that died

Beneath hurt, disappointment, anger

Despair, grief, poverty, abuse, betrayal

The you that God is reformulating

I want to be the inamorata

That tantalizes your every sense

Mentally stimulating the empty spaces

You keep hidden

Sparking curiosities in your sexuality

That cause you to forget your inhibitions

To animate your spirituality

Interlocking all three with God's divine sensual entity

Forming a bond that is surreal

And impenetrable

LOOK AT LOVE THROUGH MY EYES

To know your heart

Which is so large

That it encompasses compassion enough

To fill a football stadium

But individualized enough to the point

Of feeling the fraction of emotion

With one touch of your hand

The you that loves deeply

Feeling beyond what ordinary lovers feel

Love that permeates the

Skin tissue veins bones marrow

Where agape lives in the core of Genesis

Stretching, piercing, spreading, evolving

Through Revelation

The you of who you are

You, You intrigue me

The puzzle piece that was missing

The zig for my zag

The yen for my yang

The U for my y-o

You complete me

THE COFFEE SHOP

I was sitting in the local coffee shop reading in the corner closest to the window. It was early afternoon. Most people were at work, so the shop was very quiet. You come in and sit in my line of vision on the other side of the shop. The first time I look up, you are reading emails on your Blackberry Pearl.

Your bald head glistens in the fluorescent lights. Your Dolce & Gabbana eyewear makes you look so intellectual. Your caramel-colored skin looks as if you were kissed by the sun everyday of your life. Your athletic build tells me that you take great care of your body. Your arms speak volumes to me! You are dressed for your workout in your black tri-fit mesh top with run-fit shorts peeking from under your quick release basketball sweats. The next time I look up, you have stretched your legs out in front of you, intensely pushing buttons on your phone. I think, "Humm about 6', give or take an inch or two."

LOOK AT LOVE THROUGH MY EYES

The sales associate comes and asks me to sample the pound cake. I take a piece and ask the cost of a slice. The price is high in my opinion and she goes away. I look down at my book again, this time feeling you staring at me. When I look up, our eyes meet; I smile then go back to my book.

You get up to get your order and return to your seat, smiling. The sales associate comes to my table again with a slice of the expensive pound cake, compliments of you. I beam at you, mouthing "thank you." You lift your latte as my "you're welcome."

My text message alert gores off in my blue tooth. It's a download I know I didn't buy. I open it and it's Reuben's "Beautiful." Baffled, I look up, searching for an explanation. You flash a ubiquitous smile, tapping your blue tooth. Hmmm… paired devices! I search my media playlist and send back Trina's "I Got a Thing For You."

LOOK AT LOVE THROUGH MY EYES

I can see that you did not expect that. I see you smiling and nodding. You send back to me the Isley Brothers "Hello." I send back "Baby, Come to Me" by James Ingram and Patti Austin. Now I'm watching you. You gather your things and stride across the room to sit next to me at the table.

You talk about a gamut of subjects laughing, touching, and enjoying the ease of conversation. Time passes quickly. We notice the sun setting and our bellies growling.

"There's a restaurant next door. Let's check it out," you say.

We leave the coffee shop and go next door to the Italian restaurant. Even at dusk, the ambiance of the quaint establishment is perfect. We sit, we order, and we talk. Your voice is velvet, your intellect and wit captivating! I might be imagining it, but I feel you pulling me closer to you with the sexual timbre in your vocal tones. You gaze into my eyes, tickling my senses with your acumen of so many subjects.

The food comes, but I have this deviant desire to taste you. I see with my mind's eye you leaning in to kiss me gently, caressing my hair. I look down at my plate so that you don't see my thoughts. As if you sense the tension, you call my name. When I look up you lean into my space, nuzzling my cheek with yours. You gently place a soft kiss on my cheek. You linger, inhaling my scent. I close my eyes and enjoy your warmth and closeness. You lean back into your seat and straighten your glasses. Blushing I continue to play with the food on my plate.

Noticing me, you ask the waiter for to-go boxes.

"What are you doing?" I ask.

"Let's go to a place more private," you say.

We leave hastily, not really knowing where we are going. When we get to the parking garage we notice that we are ironically parked next to each other. We smile, looking surprised, wondering at how destiny placed us in the same place at the same time.

"Now what?" I ask.

"Come here," you say, pulling me close to you as we lean on your Hummer 3x.

Your kiss is sweet, slow, and passionate. You place your large, masculine hand through my tresses. Desire rises in both of us like flames crossing a dry desert. I look up at you and you see apprehension and worry in my expression.

"Don't worry," you say. "I'm not going to think anything about you that reduces the impression you have portrayed all day. You are a beautiful, honorable woman that deserves the world. May I give it to you?"

OK!! I am officially putty in your hands.

You lean in surrounding my face with your hands. Inside, my mind and body are fighting like gladiators dueling to the death. I know I shouldn't have a ravenous sexual encounter with you man, but it's been so long since I have felt this flood of passion I want to give into the moment.

You release me gently smiling. "Tomorrow we will do this thing correctly. Are you available for dinner?" You ask.

Of course I say yes and you promise to call to set the time and place. We part and all I can think about is batteries.

The next day I go to work floating on a cloud. I hear Jill Scott talking about cumulus types and I can relate. By lunch time I started counting down the hours left before I go to the house. My text message buzzes and I look at my phone. It's from you.

"Awaiting a delightful nite my queen."

"I know I have u beat n anticipation LOL"

"R u available 4 lunch?"

"Y don't I wk thru lunch n meet u @4?"

"Where r we meeting?"

"Let me finish wking n I'll hit u back"

I work feverishly through lunch, humming to myself. By 3:30 p.m. I pick up my phone and text you.

"Piedmont Townctr S PK Mall 7 pm"

"Intriguing!"

"Don't b late LOL!"

"Don't worry! ☺"

At 4:00 p.m. on the dot I shut everything down like I was going to cash a million dollar check. By the time I get to the car, you are calling.

"Hello."

"Are you going to be sexy tonight?"

"Baby, you are not ready for how sexy I'm going to be!"

You laugh. "I can't wait!"

"I'll see you soon."

I get home, shower, and dress slowly. I take my time making sure every detail is in place. I survey my image in the mirror, checking every nook and cranny. I think damn girl, you look good enough to eat,   if I must say so myself. And I laugh to myself. I head

back to the car   and you call again.

"What restaurant are we patronizing?"

"Brio, the reservation is in my name. You on your way now?

"Yes, Queen. I'll see you soon," and we disconnect.

My goodness your voice makes me moist! I don't know how

I'll make it through dinner. I drive like a bat out of hell to the

restaurant, blasting Raheem Devaughn's "Love Drug," relating you to

every word. "I'm a lovaholic for you...you got me hooked, I got you

sprung." I think: "You sure will be! HAHA!"

I get to the town center, park and walk toward the restaurant. I

see you standing in crisp, Carolina blue linen, looking like a clothed

Adonis. I watch you for a moment because you haven't seen me yet.

Your strong African features illuminate in the florescent lighting.

Your confident aura blasts away our surroundings, commanding the

attention of the world in your direction. Your back is turned and you sway back and forth to the rhythm of the band playing inside. Sensing

my gaze, you turn slowly. My pace shifts from a trot to a slow

deliberate swagger.

You see me. Obviously pleased with my painstaking efforts, a

broad smile engulfs your regal features. I put a little more sexy in my

prance toward the stairs in front of the restaurant. You glide down to

meet me, take my hand, and place a gentle kiss on my cheek.

You whisper, "You are ravishing."

I blush and you escort me into the dining area.

Dinner this time is very different. Our chairs are so close that I

feel the heat from your thigh against mine. You drink me in with your

eyes until you look intoxicated. You order lobster bisque and White

Oak Chardonnay, feeding me small bites to watch my lips encircle the

utensil. I can only imagine what you are thinking, judging from the

expression on your face every time I take a bite. I AM LOVING

THIS!

By the time dessert comes the sexual tension between us can be cut with a knife. You order Berry Vanilla Panna Cotta with fresh summer berries. I place some berries in my fingers and place them in your mouth. You slurp the berries from my fingers but you don't release my hand. Surprised, I giggle. You hold my left palm to your mouth with your hand, gnawing and licking the berry's juices from my hand, tickling my wrist with your tongue. It takes all I have not to scream in this place.

Obviously feeling the strain, you rise, place two bills on the table, and gently pull out my chair. You lead me to the door and we rush to the parking garage. Ironically, again we are parked beside each other again. Whimsically, we laugh and you ask, "Will you follow me?"

I say yes and we get into our cars. You lead me two streets away from the town center in the neighborhood on the left. At the second house on the left, a garage door opens with room for your car and mine. You drive in and motion for me to do the same. We get out of the cars and you pull me close to you. You hungrily kiss me and stroke my hair. We are standing in front of your Hummer. You hoist my body onto the hood of

the truck. I giggle loudly.

"May I taste you?" You say as you pull off my thong.

You don't wait for an answer. I hold onto the top grill for leverage. You slide my hips to the edge of the hood. Your tongue does magic tricks on my clitoris. You devour my essence like it was the lobster we just ate. You moan and smack like it's a full course meal. You finally massage me into climax and to your surprise, I squirt like a fountain onto your face.

You rise slowly, wiping your generously covered face, and say, "Damn, do that again!"

Embarrassed, I try to get down. You notice and gather my body into your arms. You carry me to the door of your home.

Somehow you open the door. You place me gently on the couch and say, "I have twelve inches for you if you squirt for me again."

Slyly, I say, "If you give me one inch at a time, I'll squirt all night." And the marathon begins.

ANTICIPATION

The anticipation is killing me!

To be so close to what seems like the man of my destiny

But not having touched him

Having shared so much mental intercourse

But not tasting him

Stroking his intellect

Toying with his acumen

Listening to his melodic lyrics

As he returns my words as his own

Wondering if what I sense is reality, infatuation, lust of the flesh

Or is he actually the one?

Established for me by the All Mighty before the beginning of time

Palpable, tangible, absolute

I can't help but question his authenticity

We have been conditioned to believe that

If something is too good to be true…it is!

114

LOOK AT LOVE THROUGH MY EYES

But is it?

I have never connected with anyone on such an intellectual level

Infused with explosive sexual energy

Feeling as an intelligent woman

Is this what love is suppose to be like?

Stimulation from every orifice

Mentally overwhelming, physically exhilarating

But still I wonder

The anticipation is killing me!

I wonder if he is just talking

Just spouting off rhythmic epithets

To slaughter my hopes of loving again

I can't afford another attack on my heart

I don't know if I will recover the way I should

The anticipation is killing me

I wonder if he is real

Am I dreaming about the connection I feel?

Why do I feel so empty without his voice

penetrating my inner ear?

Vibrating sounds of true sexual excitement against my tympanic membrane

I wonder if my desire to be loved is the driving force

initiating this anticipation

I just need to see him

Engulf him with my "knower"

Then I'll know!

But NOW…..the anticipation is killing me!

YOUR ARRIVAL

I saw you in my dreams at first

Tall, stoic, unimaginably handsome

Stride like one of the great Kings of old

Conquering one dynasty after another

Taking no prisoners

Leaving you mark on history itself

Then fantasy meets reality

When you step off the plane and into my arms

My heart skips a beat when you spot me in the terminal

It is as if time slows down

Allowing us to bask in the newness of we

Your aura touches me before your hand cups my face and you smile

"Beautiful just as I expected."

My smile meets yours as you kiss me

Apprehensively at first

LOOK AT LOVE THROUGH MY EYES

Then urgently

Stirring that longing that has festered

Over a two-year span of endless time

 You scoop me up into your arms

Plastering me against your 6'3" frame

Pressing my body against yours

Combining kinetic energy

Binding our minds and spirits together

Introducing your warmth to mine

The prelude to the ultimate encounter

Which unites us as one being

Your embrace speaks of never letting me go

My subliminal response is I'm not going anywhere

I feel your smile on my cheek

As you release me and I feel like I'm flying

High from your excitement

LOOK AT LOVE THROUGH MY EYES

Giddy that you're finally here

Then "what if" sets in and my mind drifts

You notice my expression and say

"One day at a time, we can make it happen"

I nod in agreeance

As you guide me into the future of pleasures unknown.

THIS IS DIFFERENT FOR ME

This is different for me

I want to be myself and show you my sensitivity

My provocative prowess

My sensuality and the indecorous side if me

But for the first time ever I am concerned about tainting your anointing

My mother always says,

"Don't love the title, love the man. He is a man first!"

I understand and respect that

Especially when I gaze into your chestnut eyes

Touch your chocolate covered skin

Taste your succulent lips

Listen to your deep masculine melodious descant

Bubbling ministry from your soul

Tickling my ears with banter

LOOK AT LOVE THROUGH MY EYES

Spouting euphemisms with pride

Assuring me that this is not a search and seizure mission on my part

You taunting me with tiny bits of pleasure

Me wanting so badly to position myself for pursuit

Then I remember the promise I made to myself.

"Be found by the man. Don't be the aggressor!"

Everything in me wants to overtake you with my love.

Not holding back on any aspect of who I am

But I don't want to overwhelm you with so much

Attention, affection, desire, and endless sexual ardor

That you turn away and never discover the inner me

The me that is sweeter than ice tea on a hot summer's day in the South

The me that laughs easily and loves deeply

The me that loves to hear you say, "You are beautiful"

Without expecting anything in return

LOOK AT LOVE THROUGH MY EYES

The me beyond the warm, sticky, pinkish part of love

But how will you see if I don't show you who I really am

This is different for me

I long to blow up your phone line

Until I finally hear those articulate intonations

Teasing me with simple delightfulness

I long to be the one you turn to after a long day

The one whose arms cradle you

Whose kisses your crave

Whose touch makes you quiver

Whose prayers lift you

And whose worship ushers you into God's presence

I long to be the face you see when you look into your own reflection

I long for you to be so deep inside me, I can feel you breathing

Mind, body, soul, and spirit linked for eternity

I long to be the one you think of when you hear THAT song

LOOK AT LOVE THROUGH MY EYES

To be the first person to whom you say Good Morning

And the last one to whom you say Good Night

I want to smother you with affection

Until you realize you love me

Like you have never loved anyone before

I want to push until you see who I am, how I am

This is different for me because I have discovered someone different

HE IS DIFFERENT

He is different

I made my list of the man I want

Prayed over it

Believing Psalm 37:4

That "He will give me the desires of my heart."

It's just difficult to fathom that

After all of the jokers, losers, manipulators and takers I have encountered that

He is different

Digital images do him no justice

His coco-colored skin radiates positive energy

His gentlemanly mannerisms

Project a level of respect for me

That makes me stand taller, smile brighter, feel sexier

His eyes sparkle with a hint of hidden sexual frustration

That is never uttered from his lips

His touch is cautious not obtrusive

Never wondering from polite distances

LOOK AT LOVE THROUGH MY EYES

His voice is masculine

With a hint of southern magnitude

His smile is subtle but can brighten the darkest sky

His lips are soft and sweet

Speaking truth and enlightenment

And with every word enunciated

I feel myself fall into his aura.

He politely asks, "How do you feel about kisses?"

I smile saying, "I love them."

Then with the grace of any African King

He caresses my face

Pulling me into himself

Kissing me

Transferring passion, longing and excitement into my being.

I greedily take all he offers

Returning to his supple lips over and over again.

He releases his magnetic hold on my mind

Repressing the urge to devour me in one bite.

He is different

LOOK AT LOVE THROUGH MY EYES

He does not rush

Even when Loquacious begins to push

His response is, "You will see" or "You'll find out"

Even "We'll have time for that"

Damn he's different!

I can feel the God in him

As we discuss his destiny and mine

How he respects my place in ministry and I respond in kind

But when we talk late at night

Like a teenager with a major crush

I close my eyes and picture all of the possibilities before us

Because he is so different.

THE SHOWER EXPERIENCE

I keep seeing this vision in my mind!:

You and I are on the beach basking in God's rays on our wet skin. You lean onto your side to look at me. You take an ice cube from your drink and drizzle cold water onto my chest. I jump as the frigid water touches my skin. You laugh. Now you have my attention.

I take off my sunglasses and I see mischief in your eyes. I toss my entire glass of water on you and run toward the ocean with you in hot pursuit. We splash in the shallow water, playfully enjoying the cool of the day. As the sun begins to set, you grab my hand and lead me to the edge of the surf. You turn me toward you and caress my face.

"You are truly my beautiful tropical sunflower," you say.

You lead me to the ocean view bungalow just off the surf. We meander to the shower and you turn on the water. I peel off my swimsuit watching you peeling of yours. I love the way the smooth chocolate texture of your skin glistens when it's wet. You step into the shower looking at me.

"Please join me," you say.

I glide to the shower and your take my hand. The water is steamy and I let it run from the top of my head, warming my body. I feel the heat of your body as you stand behind me touching. I move in closer so we both can feel the water. I turn and face you, initiating a passionate kiss. I feel desire rising between your legs and I smile in anticipation of what is to come. You gently lean me against the shower wall, spreading your legs for balance. I feel you positioning your arms on my sides and I wonder what you are doing. You bend down, gathering my body in your arms and hoisting me off the shower floor.

I giggle hysterically because no one has ever picked me up before! You maneuver my legs onto your biceps and you enter me slowly. I hold on tightly around your neck preparing for the ride!

You brace yourself against the wall, carefully keeping your balance. You only move your hips, amazingly continuing to kiss me. You moan low and guttural, making me squirt on your manhood. The rhythm of your hips increases as the water beats down upon our bodies. You stop abruptly, putting my legs down.

You tear back the shower curtain, bending me over the edge of the tub. I HOLD ON FOR DEAR LIFE! You place your knees on the edge

of the tub for leverage and your large hands in the crease of my hips. You pull my body back into your manhood repeatedly, increasing intensity. I scream in ecstasy as you pummel my G-spot. You release like a man who has been backed up for centuries. We collapse laughing at the noise we made together.

We collect ourselves and bathe each other slowly in the now lukewarm water. You give me small kisses on my cheeks as you wash my front. You turn around for me to cleanse your back. I admire

each muscle that supported us in the hulk-like shower demonstration.

The memory makes me smile.

"You like those guns don't you," you say, slyly.

 "Ummm Hummm!" I say rinsing away the soap.

You cackle and we exit the shower. We dry off and head for

the bedroom.

"You tired?" You ask.

"Why? You have something else in mind?" I ask.

Holding silk restraints and a blindfold, you say, "Yeah, I can

think of a few ideas."

I smile as my imagination runs wild.

I WONDER

I sit and wonder

What is your purpose in my life?

Seven days? Seven months? Seven years?

You came like a blaze of glory

Opening me up

Filling me up

Touching, tasting, laughing, playing

Seven Days…

God's divine number

Then POOF! You were gone

Like the flame that brought you here

Extinguished with one state of emergency

I Wonder

All of the passion I remember

Floating on the phone line

The intensity of attraction that lingers in my walls

Now I wonder

Where is that passion and intensity?

Can life have sucked away

The future we thought we could so clearly see?

Or is it my eyes that are becoming cloudy?

Mists of remembrances

Hazes of ecstasy

Wonder and amazement of God's divine connection

I wonder

Where is it now?

Long conversations reduced to nothing to say?

I KNOW LIFE HAPPENS!

Sacrifices have to be made

But what about ultimate happiness?

Seeing love "in a dream?"

Climatically, I miss you!

And I wonder now

Was I seeing the chimera of my soul mate's completion

Or was I just living the lattermost fool's paradise?

I wonder.

WHAT YOU GONNA DO?

You've got me now

What you gonna do with me?

Are you going to love me

Or mistreat me like those in the past?

Are you going to accept my love

Or take advantage of it

Leaving me lost, afraid, bewildered, ashamed?

Are you going to be passionate and affectionate

Or use my body as a dumping ground

For your worldly cares covered in sweat?

Are you going to caress my thoughts with

sweet images of future endeavors

Or beat me with my inadequacies?

Are you going to be the man God called you to be

Or are you going to shirk your responsibilities as

"priest of the house" and run

And allow me to stick my neck out?

So what will it be? You've got me now......What you gonna do with me?

JUST FRIENDS

Why why?

You're the apple of my eye

But you say let's be friends

Because mentally you're not all in

Friends?

How can we?

When your touch sends me into convulsions

Your kiss spins my world on its axis

Your voice memorizes my thoughts

Your attention and affection leave me breathless!

Fear keeps you from launching into the deep

Depths you admit you didn't think we would reach

If I could reach down into your soul and

relinquish that angst I would

But you'll just have to trust me.

Friends?

LOOK AT LOVE THROUGH MY EYES

How can I?

When you feel what I feel

Knowing that we could be the best thing

that ever happened

To either one of us.

How can I be your friend

When I've tasted your generosity

Feasted on your jovial positivity

Even dined in what your love would be like

Friends?

How can I?

After long days of lovemaking, laughter and liveliness

Sharing dreams, spirituality and family

Come on! Take the risk!

I promise I'm worth it!

For now friends, huh?

We'll see....

SPECIAL DELIVERY

The day progresses as usual. Thank God it is Friday and I am ready to leave work. At 3:00 pm the office is abuzz just before Reggie, the UPS guy, makes his appearance. The ladies in the office gloat over his 6'3" chocolate colored, bald head. He is intelligent and charming and that's all you need in an office full of women.

He comes in with his normal ruckus and I smile to myself. It's amazing what women will do for a little attention from a man. I am busy sorting piles of files so I do not look up when Reggie enters.

He quietly approaches my desk. "Excuse me Ms. Lady. I have a special delivery for you today."

I slowly look up from the paper-covered abyss to see him holding a red box. Startled, I smile and say thank you.

"You must have done something right this morning," he says.

I smile again surreptitiously, remembering the night before.

"Go away Reggie," I say, taking the box from him.

Curiosity swells inside me and I carefully open the little red box. I really do not know what to expect since he is always full of surprises – especially on Friday's. Once the box is free of packaging, I find a hotel room key and a list of instructions.

1. Go home, shower, and change. Open the box lying on the bed.

2. Follow the instructions in the box.

I see that this is going to be engaging. It always is when he has been shopping. I look at the clock and it's almost 4:30 p.m. I begin closing files and cleaning my desk, singing to myself and smiling. I have a sudden burst of exhilaration in anticipation of what he is planning. I hastily clean my work area and gather my things. I hurry to the door and push the elevator button.

"Don't hurt nobody," I hear someone from the office yell as the door opens.

I yell back, "I will!"

I reach the car, throwing my things onto the backseat. As I start

the engine, I notice one single rose on the seat. WOW! You are

really doing it up today! I turn on the radio and to my surprise I hear

your voice:

"Hello my queen. Today I have prepared a very special

adventure. Follow the instructions, sit back and enjoy. I love you, see

you soon."

"Okay! You are definitely going to get it tonight!" I think. I

drive home singing to myself again, my imagination running wild.

I enter the house running to the bathroom. I shower, and then take

my time with my hair and make-up. When I move into the bedroom, I

see a bright pink box and a suitcase partially packed and open. The

contents of the case are very interesting – the "goody bag" filled with

an assortment of toys and tasty little potions, a new Adam and Eve

covered nightie, and another red box. I open the bright pink box first

and it contains a "Hot Damn" red dress. Then I open the red box. In

the box are specific driving directions, a rose comb, instructions, and scripture: Songs of Solomon 2:10 "My lover spoke and said to me

'Arise, my darling, my beautiful one, and come with me." The

instructions: "Follow the directions to your next destination and be

prompt. See you at 8:00 p.m. Place the comb in your hair, even

though it pales to your beauty my love."

I look at my watch and it is 7:00 p.m.

I hasten to pack the necessities into the suitcase and put on the

red dress, when the doorbell rings. All I can think is NOT NOW!

NOT NOW! I run to the door and swing it open in frustration. To my

surprise a chauffeur is standing in full uniform.

"Your ride awaits, Madame, when you are ready."

My head feels light and I think: "Oh my goodness!! You are

really out doing yourself tonight!" I scurry back to the bedroom and

finish packing. I take one more look at myself and head for the door.

I give the driver the directions, hand him the bag, and he takes my

arm. He leads me to a champagne colored 1975 Rolls Royce with wood grain interior. I lean on the driver, giddy with excitement. I think I am officially going to pass out! I sit down on the back seat where there is another rose and a note: "Songs of Solomon 2:14 'Show me your face, let me hear your voice; for your voice is sweet and your face is lovely.' I am waiting for you my love."

Then my phone rings.

"Do you like the car?"

"Where are you? You have really outdone yourself!"

"Answer me: Do you like it?"

"Of course, my love."

"Sit back and enjoy. I'll see you soon, queen."

Then you are gone.

The driver tootles along as if he is wasting time but I enjoy the ride. We arrive at the Duke Mansion, directly in front of the old plantation. The driver escorts me to the double doors. I am greeted by the consigner with unexpected enthusiasm. She hands me another

rose with a note: "Songs of Solomon 2:4 'He has taken me to the

banquet hall, and his banner over me is love.' Join me in the Dowd

Suite."

I look up from the note at the beaming face of the consigner.

"Please follow me," she says.

She takes me to a private elevator with a bellman. When we get

to the room, the bellman knocks and leaves me at the door with my

bag.

"Enjoy, you look stunning." He kisses my hand and exits.

Now I am nervous! I've never been to a place this beautiful

before. What am I doing? My phone rings and I answer it.

I hear: "Come in using the room key I sent you."

"I'm nervous! What are you up too?" I ask, still talking on the

phone.

"Come in and see," you say, laughing. Then you disconnect.

LOOK AT LOVE THROUGH MY EYES

I stand at the door collecting my nerves. When I open the door I notice an assortment of rose petals everywhere. The room is aglow with candlelight scattered all over the suite. The old Victorian style room looks archaic but decadent. Of course, in all of this beauty, I'm looking for you. I am absorbing the ambiance, noticing how intricately you have planned this adventure.

Then I see you--dressed in crisp, cream linen, looking like you just stepped off of the sandy white beaches of the Caribbean. You saunter over to me, carrying two crystal flutes of bubbly. Your desire for me is reflected in the candlelight on your face, assuring me that you are pleased with my appearance. You gently kiss me and I bite your bottom lip, taking a glass from your hand.

"To what do I owe this pleasure?" I ask.

Your reply? Songs of Solomon 4: 10-11 "How delightful is your love...how much more pleasing is your love than wine, and the fragrance of your perfume than any spice. Your lips drop sweetness as the honeycomb...milk and honey are under your tongue."

You kiss me again then you whisper, "You deserve it." I realize now that if I ever doubted my love for you, you have truly dispelled all of that tonight.

You lead me to the sleeping porch where dinner has been prepared. We dine, laughing, talking, touching, and enjoying each other.

"Are you ready for dessert?" you ask.

"What do you have in mind?" I ask.

"Go put Adam and Eve to work and meet me in the bedroom."

We rise and move into the other room. I take my bag into the bathroom to change and refresh myself. When I return to the bedroom I smell the faintest scent of chocolate.

When my eyes adjust, I see you lying on your stomach, your head at the foot of the bed. Naked, your chocolate skin glistens in the candle's glow.

"Model for me," you say.

LOOK AT LOVE THROUGH MY EYES

I smile and sensually sachet in front of the bed. I can see the
longing rising in your expression. When I get to the side of the bed I
see several garbage bags taped together and fastened to the floor. I
see an assortment of fruits and a fondue pot warming chocolate sauce.
I say Songs of Solomon 4:16 "Awake north wind and come, south
wind! Blow on my garden that its fragrance may spread abroad. Let
my lover come into his garden and taste its choice fruits."

Your reply: Songs of Solomon 5:1, "I have come into my
garden… I have gathered my myrrh with my spice. I have eaten my
honeycomb and my honey."

You undress me and lay me on the bags. You place a plump
strawberry on the skewer and drench it in the bubbling chocolate.
You drizzle the liquid over my breasts and torso, making happy trails
all over my body. You painstakingly taste sweetness and skin,
carefully devouring every morsel. You drizzle chocolate onto my
thighs and watch it run between my legs. You pull the strawberry
free and place it into my mouth. As I taste the fruit, I suck the

chocolate from your fingers, teasing your appendages with my tongue. You moan at the sensation as I grab your palm and lick and bite the inside of your hand.

You kiss me then move to the lower half of my body. You lick and slurp at the chocolate on my thigh, teasing my clitoris with thumb. You stir my juices with your index. I stop you ready to return the favor. First I go to the "good bag" for my remote control surprise. I carefully place the butterfly on my clitoris and hand you the remote.

"What is this?" you ask.

"Your turn to be pleased but you can control the speed and duration of the toy. I play and you play."

You lay down on the bags and I repeat the same action you initiated. When I cover your shaft in chocolate, you spin the butterfly into action. I jump at the first buzz not expecting it and you laugh.

"Yeah I'm gonna like this one," you say. "You should have had this on during dinner."

I smile while placing you into my mouth. The sweet and salty taste of you is delightful, but I did not anticipate how difficult it would be to concentrate with the butterfly in the mix. You have the toy at its height as I come all over it and you release your essence on my neck and chest. We collapse on opposite ends of the plastic, laughing hysterically. You turn the toy on and off teasing me until I threaten your life.

You rise and move toward the bathroom. I hear water running and smell the sweet scent of jasmine. I get up and follow the aroma. You are lighting candles around the tub for two as bubbles swell in the octagon. We get into the tub; legs intertwined basking in our closeness. You open another bottle of champagne and pass me a glass. A comfortable silence between us lingers as you massage my feet.

"You ready for round two? How much water do you think we could waste on the floor in here?" you ask.

"Let's see," I say as I stroke your manhood into action.

You moan softly at the feel of my hand. I reach for the waterproof lube you conveniently left on the edge of the tub's rim. I toy with your nipples; pull you in for a slow, sensual kiss. I place the lube in your hand and turn over balancing my body on the edge of the tub.

"Feeling a little doggie tonight are we?" you say, smugly, while oiling you shaft.

"Bow wow wow baby!" I giggle.

You enter me slowly making sure you are in the right place. You methodically move back and forth, filling me completely. I rock back, meeting your thrusts as water sloshes around us. I reinforce my grip as your thrusts become more intense. You hover over my back placing your hands beside mine, holding on for dear life. You bow your head onto the tip of my spine, and the only things moving are your hips. Rhythmically you pulsate inside me, swearing with every other stroke. The warmth of your skin, the heat from the water, and the electricity of our lovemaking culminate in a very noisy, wet and satisfying end.

You don't move after you ejaculate, but linger inside me trying to regain your composure. My perineum muscle flexes as I do kegel exercises around your shaft. You squirm at the sensitivity and laugh at the sensation. We collapse into what is left of the water, which is not much.

"The housekeeper is going to be a mad somebody tomorrow," I say.

You chuckle, not moving. I sit back watching you. Chocolate covered sweetness, strong, sensitive, caring, driven, loving, and all mine. You open one eye seeing me watching you.

"You've got me hooked queen," you say. "You've got me sprung, my love," is my reply.

I MISS YOU

I miss you

I don't feel like I should but I do

I epitomize every day we spent together

Rewinding every moment of playfulness

The gravity of each tantalizing touch of ecstasy

Every jubilant release of laughter

Each juncture of awestruck splendor

You surprising me

Me astonishing you

I miss you

Really miss you

I toss and turn

Spin and unravel every sumptuous minute

Trying to figure out what went wrong

Was it I?

Timing, energy, fate, God's will?

Still I miss you

And I wonder do you miss me?

Do you still feel me deeply?

THE MEASURE OF A MAN

What is the measure of a man?

Is it the way he calls my name commanding my attention?

Or is it the softness of his touch when I have all of his?

Is it his old school sense of chivalry that boggles my mind

Mirroring my father's upbringing

Knowing deep inside of me that spoiling me

 comes from his amative being

Not from lust or physical emptiness

What is the measure of a man?

He gives himself to me and his family

Sparing nothing for himself

Pampering his princess

Yet sternly encouraging, molding

and providing everything

Emotionally, physically and spiritually

Though I look at you through rose-colored glasses

LOOK AT LOVE THROUGH MY EYES

I see clear images of the true measure of a man

One who loves completely

Labors diligently

Sacrifices daily

Speaks rationally

Listens whole-heartedly

You desire more from life and through experiences

You are redirecting destiny

Ambitious

Amorous

Affectionate

Vivacious and full of life

And you ask me why do I want a man like you?

Simply put

You embody the essence of a real man

THE VALIDITY IN CLONING

Why can't I take the best of several men

And formulate THE MAN OF MY DREAMS?!

The minister who loves the church

Works diligently in ministry

And is open to any flavor of intimacy

without inhibitions

His voice is heavenly and he's well-spoken

With the slightest hint of thug behind closed doors

BUT DON'T CALL HIM MY MAN!!

THAT IS UNGODLY!!

The banker in turn rhymes with me

Takes my poems and mirrors my thoughts with his

Role plays for hours

Masturbating with words

Warming my mind and body

LOOK AT LOVE THROUGH MY EYES

Oh but does he LIE!

LIE! LIE! LIE!

Then there is the young one

Affectionate, attentive, handsome, tall

Broke, inarticulate, jobless, living with his Momma

SIGH!!!

So....what I want is

The attentiveness and affection of the young one

The level of commitment to Kingdom,

the sexual prowess and intonation of the minister

And the intellectual stimulation of the banker

Is there one?

Or is there some validity to cloning?

DIRTY HEARTS

It is an ordinary Saturday afternoon. As usual the normal crowd has assembled at my apartment. There are five females and five males, and we have started our "left jab juice" routine. Left Jab Juice consists of whatever liquor is brought into the house being poured into one container. Most of the time it is a grayish looking liquid that sneaks up on you then punches you like Tyson's left jab; hence the name.

One of the Alpha Males says, "Let's play a game." We all perk up. He says, "This game is called Dirty Hearts. We have a deck of cards and we are each dealt one card at a time. The person with a heart in their hands gets to command one person in the room to do whatever they want them to do. If you get the Ace of Hearts, you get to command the entire room to do something."

We cast suspicious looks at each other only imagining the thoughts revolving in each other's minds.

"Shall we begin?" our Alpha Male asks.

We all sit in circle on the floor as he deals a card to everyone. Some of the people in the crowd smirk to themselves and you can almost smell the creative brain juices spouting into the air. The Alpha Male says, "Who has a heart?"

One of the females turns her card over

He asks, "What is your wish?"

She looks directly at the Alpha Male and says, "Worship me! Grovel at my feet and repeat after me."

He crawls over to her as she stands in her Queenship pose and speaks. "Say this: I am the most exquisite creature ever created by God. My juices are like the nectar of the fruits of Eden. No woman on Earth can compare to my beauty"

The Alpha Male says what she asks and we roar with laughter. He collects the cards, shuffles, and deals again. This time three people receive hearts. One female looks at me and says, "Go to the dealer and suck all of his fingers."

I smile and sprint to the kitchen grabbing a small jar of honey. I return to the circle positioning myself beside the Alpha Male. I drizzle his fingers with honey then slowly and painstakingly lick, suck, bite, and savor every one of his appendages. He moans, squeaks, giggles, and shakes. I couldn't help but notice his erection growing beneath his pants. As I place his last finger in my mouth, I fondle his manhood. He screams, "You ain't right!" The room erupts with laughter again.

The next heart belongs to a male and his request is simple. He turns to the female next to him as he commands, "Kiss me." She turns to face him and pecks his lips, but he grabs the back of her head and begins this deep, passion-filled kiss that startles the group. Tongues intertwining, heat resonating from their bodies….

He twists his fist into her hair and she literally starts rising from the floor. They are still engaged when she repositions herself and is now on all fours. She jerks herself quickly away from him escaping from his grasp. Then she starts barking like a dog! We all stare in utter amazement. Sudden gut-bursting laughter engulfs the room.

I say, "Damn, can I get a heart next? I want some a that!"

The third heart belonged to the Alpha Male. He had the ace. Here we go! The male looks at me and says, "Let's relive last night."

I look at him inquisitively.

He announces, "I have the ace! This is what we will do. Each of you ladies will be tethered to the bed and blindfolded. Each male will come into the room and do whatever they wish to you EXCEPT FUCK YOU. Foreplay only, fellas. Then the roles will be reversed. The men will be tethered then the ladies can have their way with us. Who will go first? Come my sweet and prepare the bed."

I move quickly to my room and position the tethers to the bed posts. One by one each female is tied and blindfolded to the bed and each male goes in and does his bidding. Of course we keep the door open to feed the voyeur in us all. Some give innocent kisses on thighs

and breasts. Others are bold enough to stir juices and tweak nipples.

When it is time for the male with the ace to be tethered, we plan the

cote de gras especially for him. When he is secured and blindfolded,

all of the females enter the room.

Each of us chooses a body part and goes to work. We lick

thighs, suck nipples, toy with his manhood, nibble on his stomach

until he squeals like a bitch! We enjoy every minute of it. When we

finally untie him, he reaches for my condom stash and rips the rest of

his clothes off. His manhood is elongated and fully erect.

"Brothers I don't know about you, but I think it's pussy time

right about now!" he says.

The next few minutes are a total blur of clothing and condoms

flying everywhere. Friendship lines are smeared and hot cum is

everywhere. It looks like a scene from Sodom and Gomorrah. A

female is riding the Alpha /male while another female is squatting

over his face. Out of the corner of my eye I see one male holding a female in the air. Her legs are wrapped around his arms and he is bouncing her up and down on his massive manhood. My vision blurs quickly when another King Dong is thrust in my face. Of course I place it in my mouth and do what I do best. While I am working, I am bent over by a huge hand on my back. The male behind me eases his shaft into my dripping wet orifice and slowly strokes while I continue to suck the shaft in my mouth. The female that was on the face of the Alpha male, jumps from the bed to join us. She takes the shaft from my mouth, covers it with a condom and takes the male away. The male behind me gets impatient and lifts me from the ground. I wrap my legs around his body and brace myself against the wall. He continues to penetrate my body from behind, bouncing and spinning his pelvis in circles. I am so wet, my pussy sounds like a washer on spin cycle.

The entire room is filled with lascivious laughter, moans of ecstasy, and total amusement. The excitement dulls to a low hum and we lay wherever we are, spent and amazed. Someone says, "I need a bath." We look around at each other, but no one moves quickly. I find some energy from somewhere and move toward the bathroom first. Slowly, all ten of us file into the standard shower to bathe. ALL OF US! We line up male/female, soaping, touching, enjoying the strange closeness we have just developed. We change positions, allowing everyone an opportunity to be close to the water. We get out, dry each other off, play with lotion for everyone, redress, and move back to the circle on the floor. My roommate helps me clean up my room, strip the bed and light incenses. No one really speaks. We smile and touch each other in passing. I go to the kitchen for another drink and to start cooking.

Someone asks, "What shall we play next?" Laughter reverberates again!

WORDS

It's so amazing

How words can affect you

As kids we said, "Sticks and stones can break our bones but

words will never harm me."

But that's a lie!

Words cut deeper than a two-edged sword

Or they heal like an ointment on an open wound

Words can build an ego to mammoth proportions

Or tear down self-esteem

Until you feel your soul scraping the dirt

Words tickle the senses

Entice emotion

Invoke desire and admiration

Words develop hope

You and I have exchanged a cacophony of words

Words of interest

Cordial intercourse

That has lead us to this place

Has it even been a month?

And yet it seems like an eternity

Feasting on your words.

But where are your actions?

LOOK AT LOVE THROUGH MY EYES

You say you love me

But your calls are sporadic

You are on your way to see me

But three days later

I go on a scavenger hunt to find you

Your excuse?

Just WORDS!

You say God sent me to you

WORDS!

You say you long to touch me

WORDS!

You say you are ready for me completely

WORDS! WORDS! WORDS!

I cling to these adjectives, hyperboles,

personification, onomatopoeia

Still, when I close my eyes

And reach out my hands

Feeling the intensity of my thoughts

And imagining verbs floating in the atmosphere

Irrevocable deeds never experienced

Wanting to feel taste touch manifested reality

and getting nothing

Why? It's because of your inexplicable seducing words.

DECEPTION, LIES, UNTRUTH

Deception, lies, untruth

Do I unwillingly invite these demons into my life?

What is it in me that attracts such deceit?

Do I contrarily open myself up to be subjected to detrimental

treatment?

What is it that draws me into lyrical symphonies of

enchantment?

Rapturous words surrounded with hopefulness, optimism,

promises, moxie,

Only to lead to disappointment, misfortune, displeasure,

bitterness, despair

Was it something I said?

Was I too assertive again?

Should I have not mentioned my desire to please and fulfill?

Should I have kept my thoughts of admiration, attraction,

entreaty to myself?

All I want is love in return

To give unlimited affection

To smother him with endearment that is immeasurable and
never ending.
To be loved unconditionally
Intellectually exhilarated
Physically enticed
Spiritually compatible
Adored and spoiled to the core.

Deception, lies, untruth
Maybe I need to stay away from the smart ones
But can I live without the mind freak?
Can I deal with no stimulation surrounding
my cerebral cortex?
To what end?
To settle for physical pleasure that won't
work without mental stimulation?
Can I live with dead conversations
Having to explain myself after every word
That is not living and it won't be love.

Deception, lies, untruth
Somewhere there is a beloved reality for me
Beyond those eloquent words.

LIES

Here I go again

Falling

For melodious symphonic lyrics

Of love, lust, passion and lies

LIES! LIES! LIES!

Why must most men lie?

What pleasures do weak-minded individuals gain

From painting portraits

Of unconditional love and support?

A home full of laughter, happiness and ecstasy

Days glittered with spontaneity

Nights enamored with quiet conversations, long walks

And uninhibited intimate encounters

Rooms cluttered with toys

From the little miracles God blessed us with.

LOOK AT LOVE THROUGH MY EYES

Long drives to visit relatives

Holidays spent smothered in the joy of family.

LIES! LIES! LIES!

Rekindling deceit and bitterness

I thought I had released with my old name..

Now I'm nursing the same scar again,

A freshly opened wound

Seeping from my subconscious

Slowly making new roots in my being.

I can feel it leeching onto the places

I left open for someone new,

Hardening the soft areas in which passion once lived,

Creeping into my conscious thoughts,,

Battering my self-image

Release this fool from the uttermost places in your heart!

Pull his seducing masculinity away for your expectations.

LOOK AT LOVE THROUGH MY EYES

Pretend you did not embrace his manliness

And bask in his aura.

Imagine you did not feel anything

When he blasphemed against your God

Claiming you were sent to him as his helpmate

Shut out the thoughts of his ministry

Intertwining with yours

And allowing the Most High

To use such a union for Kingdom work.

Focus instead on his sporadic calls,

His night time disappearing acts

And his LIES!!!

I wish I did not long for such a man,

One who seemingly has life in the palm of his hand.

All he needed was me

Or is that the lie to end all lies?

THE PORCH

It is a steamy Sunday afternoon. The weatherman said it is 103 degrees and it is three o'clock. We got a break from evening service, which does not happen often. Your Mom wants to visit with her "grandbabies," giving us an evening together to spend quality time.

I cook dinner: salads with chicken--and strawberry shortcake. After dinner we venture to the porch, which faces the Charleston Harbor. Thank God for the wind blowing toward the house. When the baby was born, you bought us matching swivel rockers so that we could cradle the small ones in the sunshine. Now the two of us sit in comfortable silence, enjoying each other's company. I lean back, closing my eyes and savoring the breeze. I feel you watching me. You gently wipe perspiration from my brow.

"You shol is a pretty gal," you say in an exaggerated Southern drawl.

"Well that shol is nice of you to say sir," I say mimicking your dialect.

I'm wearing a tank top and a peasant skirt. You have on a tank and basketball shorts. Both of us are barefoot. "Voyage to Atlantis" by the Isley Brothers blasts from the living room. You dip your fingers into your lemonade, removing an ice cube. You drizzle cold wetness down my arm. My reflexes react suddenly and then relax.

"That feels wonderful!" I say.

Our chairs are close enough for me to touch you. I reach my left arm out, searching for your manhood. I find my mark and massage you into attention.

"He's awake, now what you gone do?" you ask.

I giggle and jump off my rocker. I lean over you, passionately kissing your lips. I straddle your chair, grinding your private area. You pop my breasts over the top of my tank, caressing them with your hands continuing to kiss me. You reach down under my large skirt to

170

touch my wetness. You twirl your fingers around, feeling the flow of my essence. You remove your fingers and place them in my mouth. I taste sweet and salty.

You hungrily take my kisses as I share my essence with you. I pull your manhood from your shorts, stroking to ensure an ultimate erection. I turn my body around with my back to you, lifting my skirt up to my waist. I maneuver your manliness into my wet orifice. First I move slowly to the rhythm of "Sexual Healing" by Marvin Gaye. I swivel my hips in hula hoop circles as you move the rocker so that you penetrate me deeply. You moan in ecstasy. My pace increases until I am bouncing and grinding with new found intensity. I hold on to the arms of the rocker to keep my balance.

"You better work that ass girl!" You shout and smack my right butt cheek.

I smile to myself. I work until you grab my hips, directing me into your climax. You release wildly, pulling me so close I can feel your stream of wetness squirting inside of me. You rest awhile,

enjoying our union. I move my muscles and you react lovingly.

When I get up, you say, "I'll race you to the shower." I take

off running, anticipating another encounter.

DEATH OF MARRIAGE

My marriage died first

Not a horrible kicking and screaming death

But a slow leaky kind of death

You know

When you can sense something is wrong

But you patch it with

Sex and shallow conversation

Planning to spend time together

But never meeting in the same room

It's over now

For me anyway

What I don't understand is

Why are you trying so hard now?

You did not want me three weeks ago

Now you call every hour

Texting me to death

And to accomplish WHAT?!!!

LOOK AT LOVE THROUGH MY EYES

Have you changed your mind about babies?

Have you decided that I'm worthy of spending some time with?

Or are you just horny and miss

The good loving I always could supply?

What do you want from me?

I gave you everything

But that wasn't enough for you!

I'm moving on with my life and soon

With love!

THE THINGS I LONG FOR

Oh how I long to feel

Your embrace after you enter my door.

Your masculinity surrounding me,

Giving comfort, protection, and strength.

I long for the soft, supple feel of your kiss

That lingers even when you let go.

I long for your hands to surround my face

As you move in more passionately, kissing

Feeling the excitement, electricity surging

From your finger tips, pulsating through me.

I long to see the smile that comes

Ever so slowly to your lips

That all knowing, confident, arrogance

That beams with intelligence, desire, and wittiness

Knowing you can have, but don't desire to intrude upon

The things so willingly given.

I long to feel your hands kneading, probing places

LOOK AT LOVE THROUGH MY EYES

That haven't been touched in awhile

Exploring hidden crevices and tight short spaces

I long to feel the touch of your tongue

On the tip of my desire

Taking, giving, teasing and tapping

Tasting small pieces of my innermost being

Without greedily devouring

Each essential part that's me

I long to taste the essence of you

Not only the lava from your

Throbbing, permeating volcanic eruptions,

But the parts of you that you keep hidden.

The true depth, width, length, and breadth of you

That sits in the core of your soul

Keeping the fire ignited in your spirit

The "mysterium tremendum" of who you are.

LOOK AT LOVE THROUGH MY EYES

Umm to taste your

Lipsneckfingerstorsothighskneesandback

Landing ultimately on the "happy trail"

Pleasing you until your toes curl,

Hairs stand up straight

Leaving you to whimper my name.

I long to love you

Not surface superficial Valentine's Day love

But deep, intense, forever kinda love

The kinda drugged out love

That will make a sista drive to Timbuktu

Just to see the light in your eyes

The kinda love that makes you tell folks you don't know

Why God has blessed you so richly

With someone that thinks for himself,

Doesn't live with Momma,

And can talk in complete sentences.

Best of all he has a job!

The kinda love you feel deep inside

Beyond your heart

LOOK AT LOVE THROUGH MY EYES

Seeping into the core of epiphany…

Restful, caring, compassionate love

TRUE through and through

Oh how I long for you!

KIDNAPPED

It's been three months since we were together. Though time passes quickly, it seems like an eternity. You suggested that I pack a bag and bring it to work today. Without question I do it, wondering what you are planning. You surprise me on my way to work with a phone call. I am elated! I love it when I am the first thought on your mind so early in the morning. I smile to myself as I drive into work.

The day progresses without incident. As I head to my car, my phone rings.

"Hello?"

"Let's pretend that you are walking to your car and you notice a white van following you. Don't be afraid, I'm in control today. Do I have your permission to play?" you ask.

"Proceed," I say. You disconnect.

Suddenly, the van pulls up and two guys jump out. One guy takes my purse and the other pushes me into the van. The door closes and I'm blindfolded with my hands bound in front of me. We speed off, and I hear my car start up and follow us. No one talks to me and my heart is racing, but I smell the faintest scent of cigarettes. We drive for what seems like twenty minutes and come to a stop. The door opens and I am encouraged to exit the van. I am escorted across a concrete lot, judging from the sound beneath my feet. Someone puts my purse strap in my bound hands.

"Your keys are inside your bag ma'am. I'm going to take you to a chair and you have been asked to wait."

I hear what seems to be an old rickety, metal door open then close. Tap, tap, tap go my shoes and the shoes of my escorts. I feel the chair on the back of my legs when the escort places me before it. He unties my hands as I sit in the chair. He restrains me again to a high back velvety feeling chair, one wrist on each armrest. I am still blind folded, listening.

The man leaves and my senses begin to magnify. I hear a fan running in the distance and the familiar mixture of aromas waft past my nostrils. Jasmine incense, chocolate sauce, a sweet wine? Interesting.....My heart begins to pound again when I hear footsteps moving toward me.

The stride of the gait sounds like you are approaching. You stop fifteen feet in front of me and I hear a camera flash. I don't speak because you haven't given me any directions, but my mind is reeling! You come closer to me, smelling like a man scented by Heaven, and you untie the blindfold. You back up to look at me.

First my focus is on you – dressed in a navy Ralph Lauren Purple Label suit, coupled with a Ralph Lauren Black Label Bond Solid baby blue, French cuffed shirt that is perfectly tailored to fit your muscular frame. Your accents are a Ralph Lauren Museum Paisley silk tie, a pair of blue tipped Cole Haan Air Ludlow loafers, and blue finished Tiffany Basket Weave cuff links, making your outfit perfectly complete.

181

You are smiling ever so coyly at me. I return your smile then I begin to take in my surroundings. You have established a room of extreme fantasy. You step aside as I gawk at the different stations you have arranged. I have never seen any of these things before. OMG!

"Hello sexy. How was your day?" you say.

"Obviously getting more interesting by the minute," I say.

You chuckle. "The boys didn't hurt you, did they?"

"No, but I was scared out of my mind!"

You laugh again.

"You hungry?"

"I could eat."

"Listen carefully. Through those doors to the left is a shower. Freshen up and don the clothes I've prepared for you and come to the table. I'll be waiting for you."

LOOK AT LOVE THROUGH MY EYES

You release my restraints and I rise from what I now know as the "Throne" and I walk toward the door, as you instructed. When I open the door I find a standard work shower with no frills at all. I do see a small box of scented soaps and lotions, all of which are your favorites. I smile at your attention to detail. I shower, thinking of all of the possibilities for tonight. I dry off, lotion up, and look for my attire for the evening. There is one locker standing open to my right. As I approach, I see my thigh high boots and a crotchless, fishnet bodysuit. Interesting night indeed!

I dress slowly and deliberately, pulling my hair back into a ponytail. I carefully apply my makeup in a smoky design, glossing my lips 'til they POP! You supplied a short Kimono robe for me to wear for dinner. I triple check myself in the mirror before I exit the shower area. I open the door to see you sitting on the Throne. You rise and we meet in the middle of the floor.

"I'm going to have to pray to get through dinner," you say.

I smirk and say, "I'm pleased you approve, my love."

"Yes, beautiful, very much so!"

You escort me to a table covered in finger foods. Every course is cut into small portions so that we have to feed each other the meal. There are no utensils, just bamboo skewers of all shapes and sizes. We sit and dine, laughing, talking, teasing, tasting, and enjoying each other's company. When dinner is done, you stand up, taking my hand and pulling me to my feet. When I stand you remove my robe smiling.

"Listen carefully," you say. "When you have had enough you say STOP. When you want to take a break say BREAK, and when you want more you say MORE PLEASE."

I give you an inquisitive look and you say, "Remember STOP, BREAK, and MORE PLEASE."

As we talk, you lead me toward a chair that has restraints everywhere and a very straight back. There are armrests with straps that stick out on both sides of the chair. There are chair legs that are elongated in front of it with straps to hold down my thighs. You tell me that it is called the Erotic Recliner. Beside it, there is a machine with the mold of your manhood protruding from the tip of it. I've seen this type of machine on the *Bunny Ranch* from TV. You tell me it is called the Fucking Machine. I give you a look of astonishment and your smile broadens. I shake my head and wonder what the hell I have gotten myself into.

"I'll go slowly; I won't turn it up until you say more," you say.

I concede and take my position on the Erotic Recliner. You strap me into the recliner, positioning the machine you have named the Titan. I hear my heart beating inside my head as you take a seat in front of me with the touch screen remote at the ready.

"Oh let me help you!" you say.

We are like virgins bumping in the dark with this adventure! You walk in front of me and kneel down, gently caressing my clitoris. I can never figure out why your fingers feel better than mine. You stir my juices, enjoying the fact that I can't move. I look down at your kid-in-a-candy-store expression just as you plunge your face into my essence.

I cry out in surprise as you flick and lick the warmest part of me. Just as I rest my head back against the headrest of the chair, you start wiping your face with a towel that is close by. You push the phallic shape inside my walls then take your seat again.

"You ready?" you ask.

You push the remote and the penis moves slowly, oscillating inside me.

"More please," I say.

"Okay, let's see what this thing can do," you say.

You begin pushing buttons and the toy goes crazy. It feels like it is literally jumping inside of me. The vibration is so intense I pull at the restraints to get away. I look at you like a deer in head lights; my mind goes blank, forgetting the code words. I feel an immeasurable orgasm surging through my hair follicles, stretching into every limb, muscle, vein, bone marrow. I bob up and down until a scream is released from my throat that starts in my toe nails. I jerk, quiver and twitch with tears streaming down my cheeks through this unbelievable sensation.

I look down to see a creamy mess all over the machine. You stop it, marveling at the transformation I've gone through. You approach me to free me of the restraints and I notice an erection of enormous proportions in your pants.

I try to stop the trembling and steady my breathing but it is a struggle. You release me and pull me from the machine by the waist. I climb you as if you were a tree and I straddle your body, while you thread my hair into your fingers pulling my neck back, giving my jugular your complete attention. You hold me up by my butt cheeks, carrying me to the next apparatus. I'm so wet from the machine that you feel my essence on my thighs through the fishnets.

LOOK AT LOVE THROUGH MY EYES

You carry me to a queen size Excel canopy bed with a wrought

iron headboard, fitted with a black sheet. The bars are exposed

and there are some interesting "tools" on and around the bed. Draped

on the headboard are tethers connected to strict leather, fur-trimmed

locking restraints for my wrists, a Penetration Station, and a Sex

Wedge. You place me gently on the side of the bed and I look around

at all of these things.

"Do you know what you're doing with this stuff?" I ask.

You smile and say, "I read the instructions and researched

them online. We will learn together. Now lean back and play with

your wetness and watch me undress."

I prop my boots up on the bed and run my fingers along my

clitoris and vulva. You peel off your clothes watching me intently.

I dip my fingers into my stickiness, place my fingers in my mouth to

taste my juices, and close my eyes. Then I feel you moving closer

to me and I open my eyes to see you buck naked standing in front of

me. Your penis is bulging, bouncing and erect.

When you reach me, you grab the crotchless hole, ripping it to make it even bigger. I giggle with excitement. You instruct me to position myself in the middle of the bed, spread eagle. As I comply, you place my legs in the Penetration Station straps and cuff my arms over my head with the fur-lined restraints. I look down at you through my arms and you have this hungry look in your eyes.

You are shaking a can of sugar free whipped cream while crawling onto the bed. You cover my vagina and ass in white, creamy foam. I feel like I'm watching you in slow motion as you lick and slurp and bite my inner thighs. When you finally get to my vagina, you painstakingly taste the cream which is intermingled with my essence. You pay special attention to my clitoris, flicking it with your tongue. Then you tilt my hips upward, savoring my juicy vulva, sticking your tongue in and out of me, simultaneously tossing my salad. My legs shake as I feel an orgasm coming on.

"Back up or you'll get squirted on!" I yell.

"Give it to me baby."

LOOK AT LOVE THROUGH MY EYES

I try to stop the sensation, but the harder I try the worse it gets!

I feel my pelvis shudder then gussssshh!! I tremble as I release.

You lay there in front of me receiving a full frontal assault.

"Yeah baby WoooHoooo!!" you exclaim. Your head rises

from between my thighs and your face looks like a huge glazed donut.

I hold my head back, laughing and embarrassed at the same time.

You wipe your face with a towel you have nearby, and you

slide the Sex Wedge underneath my bottom. You move the

Penetration Station straps down to my thighs, adjusting the straps so

that my legs are stationary. You remove the pillows from around

my head and you stand over me looking like Apollo basking in the

glory of a victorious war. You straddle my thighs and squat "froggy"

style over me. You glide your manhood into my tilted body, holding

my thighs for leverage. Your manhood glistens as you move in and

out in a steady motion.

"Oh shit, it is so wet!" you holler.

I look at you making those ecstatic facial expressions, enjoying our union. I pull at the restraints because I am aching to touch you.

I yell, "STOP!"

You look up at me confused.

"Please release my hands, I want to touch you," I say.

You smile, slyly and say, "Not yet."

You continue this slow, grinding torture as your shaft thickens, filling me completely. I scream in frustration, which seems to excite you even the more. You transition into the missionary position, pulling the straps on my legs upward to my ankles, extending my legs. You place your hands on me in the bend at my thighs, close to my belly. With every thrust I feel like you may puncture a lung! You reach for the straps on the bed, which allow you even deeper penetration IF THAT'S EVEN POSSIBLE!

I moan a loud, agonizing sound as you pound that pussy into cat litter. I can feel your penis head pounding my G and I feel that sensation again. Before I can warn you--gussssssshh! I squirt cum and wail all at the same time. Your smile is as wide as the Nile. You stop, release my restraints, and unfasten and remove my boots. You command me to turn over. I DON'T THINK I CAN TAKE ANYMORE!

As I reposition myself, you place the straps you were holding in my hands and tell me to hold on. You put the Sex Wedge under my hips in doggie style position. You glide your manhood into my wetness and begin again.

Once you establish your rhythm, you spank that ass saying, "Whose pussy is this?"

"Yours, Big Daddy. Yours!" I answer.

You spank me again, leaving that expert sting; then your intensity increases and I know what time it is. You grab my hips with renewed fervor until a rumble that is akin to Shaka Zulu's battle cry is released from your inner most being. You collapse heavily on my back, your sweat merging with mine, your seed mingling with my essence.

We lay there for a moment relishing our new experiences. You roll over onto the bed and we burst into laughter.

You say, "One day, these new experiences are going to get the best of us." I look at you and say, "Would you want to go any other way?" You smile at me and start flailing things from off the bed. You reach beside the bed, recovering the pillows and blanket. You toss the covers over us and cocoon my body into your arms. You kiss my temple and say, "You are one crazy chick you know that?" "And that's why you love me," I say. Just that quickly, I hear the faintest sound of you sleeping. I nuzzle your neck and cuddle closer to you, imagining our next adventure.

I KNOW WHAT I WANT

For the first time in my life

I sat and gazed into the eyes of

A different kind of man

For hours we sat and discussed

Major and minor controversies:

Homosexuality and lesbianism

The truth about Lot's wife

Amusement parks

Misappropriation of evangelical funds

Suspense motives, psychotic storylines

Subtle hints of sexuality

Quickly redirected with hilarity

Marriage – to do, or not to do

A gamut of subjects

Entertaining, intellectual, free-spirited,

attentive, anointed

But this was different

And I know the change is in me

I realize what I want

I was like a sponge

Gleaning from every enunciated syllable

falling from his full succulent lips

My ears tingled with every crescendo

and decrescendo of his vocal inflections

How he pauses between words to make a point

How he laughs openly and easily

To invite conversation, encouraging comfort

And with every question asked

There is a moment of reflection proceeding articulation

Meditation of the right phrase to say

To ensure the correct response

And provoke counter argument

Ahh, but the crème de la crème is his face

Sincerity, honesty, disbelief, compassion, energy

Vigilant Intensity!

Every inflection had an expression

The longer we had verbal intercourse

The more enraptured I was in a blaze of hazel enchantment

And I realized what I want

Imagining myself watching him in his element

Among the stars with whom he is destined to be

Eavesdropping on bits of conversation

Seeing the glow of his integrity standing out from among them

LOOK AT LOVE THROUGH MY EYES

Visualizing his sun-kissed skin basking in the tropical horizon

Stealing the attention from God's purest Earth

Listening to him dote over his niece

Conceptualizing him as a father

And I realized what I want

"What made this man different?" you ask.

There was no sexual tension between us

He genuinely gave me his full attention

Not wanting anything in return

His phone rang INCESSANTLY!!

But he focused on me

He listened to what I said

Without analyzing my faults

And I realized what I want

We connected on a level that I have never experienced

Kinetic energy adjoining spiritual prowess

Causing the anointing inside of me

To spark a divergent flame

Mirroring the gleam from his eyes

Fortifying sanctification and holiness

Without being ostentatious

Refreshing! He was so refreshing!

All I had to do was be who I am!

And I realize what I really, truly, honestly want…

A TRUE MAN OF GOD!

I NEVER EXPECTED IT

I never expected it

Falling in love again

I prayed for it

Dreamed of loving touching holding

Someone who truly loves me

Someone who could match my assertive sexual prowess

But refrains and admires my enthusiasm to please him

Someone who loves words as much as I do

Tossing phrases back and forth

Mirroring my intellect and wittiness

Someone who loves God as much as me

And longs to work WITH me in ministry

Instead of feeling like he's sharing me with the church

Someone so connected with me spiritually

That I can feel his love moving across space and time

He understands that I am not perfect

And loves me beyond my faults

The rabid beast that torments him

LOOK AT LOVE THROUGH MY EYES

Is soothed by God's praise in the inflections of my voice

His love is genuine

Not manufactured from lustful desires

Or lascivious residue from the night before

His love for me feels different

Launching out in the depths of faith enough

To profess amore that encompasses us both

His love reaches into my heart

Massaging away doubt, disappointment,

false promises, and bullshit from my past

Pressing in God's love intermingled with his own

Causing me to ask again: Could this be it?

I told him I am afraid to give myself to him completely

His reply, "I will love enough for both of us until you're ready."

WOW!!!

I do love him

Not for what he can do for me

but for what he is allowing God to do for us

LOOK AT LOVE THROUGH MY EYES

He is so full of compassion that his soul aches for humanity's injustices

He is so full of passion that his naughty thoughts make my vulva leap in anticipation

He hungers for so much more of God that his ministry screams from his testimony

I love him because he loves me

Not just for my physiology or my dominant personality

But he loves the me that God is formulating

I never expected it! But now it's here.....

True love!

PURGATORY

I've never been to a party like this. I carefully planned my

outfit, my hair, and my make-up. I have always been interested in the

world of fetish, but never thought I'd have an opportunity to be "Lady

Heather." Dressed in a black fishnet shirt, large fence net pantyhose,

a wet look skirt and four-inch, thigh high boots, I mount the sidewalk

approaching Purgatory. I love new experiences but I must admit

that I am very nervous. I have always wanted to explore the side of

me I suppress so often, but damn it I look sexy as hell!

There are explicit rules I had to learn before attending this

Fetish Party. The theme for the party is medical so people are to

dress in something reflecting the medical profession. No female

nipples or genitalia can be shown at any time, and all sexual activity is

prohibited; but I still was not prepared for what I was about to see!

As I walk into the venue I am inundated with sensual

stimulation. I wait in line to walk the "Red Carpet" where beneath

the velvety redness are men waiting to be stomped on by stiletto, wedge, and chunky heels of different proportions. I am led to the

carpet cat walk by a masked punisher and he holds my hand for

leverage. Designated photographers snap pictures and I really give

them my Naomi Campbell walk!

On cloud nine now, I walk to the bar and order a drink. I stand

in the middle of the room taking in the scenery. People are in all

types of undress. A fair skinned, tall woman has on a white thong,

thigh high boots, nipple covers and a surgical mask. THAT'S IT!

Another woman has wrapped herself in gauze from head to toe.

There is a man dancing around with a cape, a thong, and combat

boots. Simulated surgeries are being performed on stage with gushing

blood and comical story lines. I notice some of my acquaintances are

dancing on different podiums as the techno music thumps to keep

the energy high in the room.

What a scene! A female in a smoking black and white

leather corset saunters over to me. "This is your first time," she says

"Is it that obvious?" I say.

"Come, let's go to VIP. There are some real goodies up there." She strides toward the stairs and as I watch her walk I swear she is the sexiest big, beautiful white girl alive!

We venture up the stairs past various vendors selling an assortment of collars, cuffs, and instruments of torturous pleasure. The first station is the work place of Dr. Spankenstein, who is wielding devices of painful delights such as hot wax and low voltage shock treatment. I am surprised at how excited I get watching a plus sized female enjoying the sensual touch of electricity.

In the second station, I see him–Black Adonis. Covered in a black X-harness, studded and spiked from shoulder to shoulder, he expertly HANDLED the spanking apparatus with this tiny customer. I watch entranced by the stealth of his movements. He begins by removing her miniskirt, exposing her black thong. She faces the bonding cross and he straps her to it by the wrists, restricting her movements. He turns to pick up a spur, looking directly into my eyes.

He smiles at the astonishment in my expression, appraising and admiring my attire. Then he turns back to his customer and seemingly performs just for me.

He caresses her left butt cheek slowly then spanks her with his massive caramel colored hand. The sound resonates through me and he notices. He surreptitiously looks back at me and spanks her again. He chooses his next instrument of pleasure by placing a spur in his hand, running it over her exposed back. He switches again, wielding a glove covered on one side with kid skin and the other with fur. He caresses her body while stealing glances at me the entire time. Once he finished with her, he unbinds her and she redresses.

He faces the crowd watching, asking for the next customer. His gaze is on me, his eyes inviting me into this workshop he has created. I can't move! I feel like everything has disappeared except for the two of us. Reality sets in when my sexy escort suggests that we move to the next booth. I shake off the trance and move on with her. We wander around, watching the flogging and rope suspension swing high into the air. I can feeling the wind from

the body swinging on the rope suspension's momentum.

I am standing by the railing watching the crowd dancing,

kissing, touching; just enjoying the freedom of the atmosphere.

I lost the escort in the corset somewhere in the bar traffic.   I close my

eyes, inhaling the rhythm of the music, when I feel two large hands on

my shoulders. I slowly turn to face "Adonis."

"I saw how intrigued you were with my station. May I show

you more? I'd like to make sure that no one steals you away," he

says, handing me a collar with a C-ring for a leash.

I ask, "What will this do?"

He answers, "It will let everyone know that you are taken."

I hesitate, unsure of what I am inviting into my personal space.

I say, "Okay, but I am a novice so be gentle with me."

"My pleasure," he says with that sexy, mysterious smile.

LOOK AT LOVE THROUGH MY EYES

He places the collar on my neck, mentally taking me to a whole

new world. Unexpectedly, he attaches a leash to the C-ring. He

carefully watches my expression, testing his parameters, gently

pulling me to follow him. My heart is beating 1,000 beats per minute!

My mind is reeling with excitement, anticipation, terror, and

uncertainty.

He leads me to a quiet space where couches were placed

for   intimate conversations. We talk, laugh, touch, kiss, caress,

and spend time exploring each other mentally and physically.

He teaches me words we will use for "stop," "more," and "go."

He teaches me things I need to know as a submissive. Of course

I immediately ask, "When the roles switch, what words do I use?"

He heartily laughs at my spunkiness and forward approach to life,

qualities he says he admires.

An announcement is made for last call and he turns to me.

"Shall our adventure continue now?"

I sigh heavily. Internally I am torn, though every fiber of my being screams YES YES YES!!!!

Seeing the hesitancy in my face, he says, "What is the difference between sharing yourself with me now or six months from now? You will be the same sensual, sexy, alluring, intelligent woman I see now."

I think: THAT'S IT, YOU CAN GET IT!! Why am I such a sucker for the gift of gab? I concede and he leads me to the parking lot. He releases me from the leash and follows me to my car.

He says, "The key is for you to be more comfortable. If this is too much for one night, I can understand."

I say, "I need a release after all of this excitement. Toys won't do it for me tonight."

He leans his 6'4" frame down to passionately kiss me. "I'll drive around to meet you and you can follow me," he says.

I watch his sexy stride as he crosses the parking lot to his car. I hurriedly get into my car, hyperventilating. Man, his kisses take my breath away! I reach and touch the collar that is still around my neck. What the hell have I gotten myself into now?

A silver Mercedes Benz E320 with tinted windows stops in front of my car. He rolls down the window and signals for me to follow him. We wheel around the corner to the Westin Hotel. He says that I might be more comfortable in a neutral place. I send a quick text to my friends, telling them where I am just in case something goes awry. When we get to the room, I sit on the bed feeling like a high school virgin preparing for her first sexual experience.

He takes off all of my clothes with an amazing sense of comfort. The intensity from his stare is burning a hole in my retina. He strides over and stands directly in front of me.

"Do I still have your permission to be dominant?" he asks.

LOOK AT LOVE THROUGH MY EYES

As I gaze up into the face of this demigod, his nearness starts a forest fire that spreads from my vulva to my skull. How can I say no? Hell I can't even speak! He smiles, genuinely, pulling me to my feet. He undresses me with a gentleness I've never experienced. With every inch of my skin exposed, he savors me with his eyes, as if memorizing every curve.

"You will bathe with me," he says, guiding me to the bathroom shower. He turns back to me after handing me exfoliating bathing gloves and foaming bath wash. I feel nervousness twisting with desire inside of me as I scrub his back.

The soap smells heavenly of herbs, causing a heady sensation. He stretches out his arms to balance himself on the shower walls, letting the water bead down his back. His muscles glisten under the soap and steamy waves of water. He bows his head so that the water runs down his back and onto me. My mind is transported into another realm just thinking that a man so majestic wants me in his presence – touching, tasting, loving.

He turns and squirts soap into his massive palms and begins to massage my body from the front. He squats and massages my legs, spinning me around so he can focus on the back of me. His hands knead my back in a circular motion, easing the tension I'm feeling. I'm putty in his hands, enjoying every minute. He pulls me into the stream of water, rinsing us both. We bathe in silence, mainly because I'm speechless. He turns off the water and we exit the tub. I grab a towel and I stand on the toilet to dry him off. He turns to watch me work with this omniscient smile. I ask, "Why me?"

He takes another towel from the rack and begins to return the favor, not allowing me to come down from the top of the stool. He says, "What is life without adventure? Besides as beautiful as you are, I didn't want anyone else to have you."

He leads me to the bedroom and pulls the bedspread down exposing crisp white sheets. He drapes silk scarves around the posts of the headboard, tying a knot at the base to keep them from slipping.

He commands me to lie down. I take a deep breath and think to myself, "and so it begins."

He ties me to the bed face down, reminding me of our code words. I bury my face in the heavenly pillows and I feel my body begin to shake. He lightly touches me with his massive hands. I stifle moans, not sure if it is acceptable to release them. I can feel the electricity from his aura penetrating through my skin right to the marrow in my bones. The sensation changes and I look back to see a huge feather tickling my senses. The tactility is unbearable and I put my face into the pillow, screaming... And he doesn't say anything. Then I feel a warm liquid running from the nape of my neck to the tip of my behind. He jumps on the bed, straddling my body. His hands begin at my shoulders, kneading every muscle. He intentionally touches every inch of my body, not leaving a spot of my skin untouched. My body shivers and I realize that I have never been touched in this way before. He leans forward and begins kissing every place his hands touch.

He works methodically, tasting every piece of muscle and skin. He works the tip of my spine, moving down to my sides, doing acrobatics with his tongue. My body violently convulses as he licks and sucks around my bottom, parting my legs. I begin kicking my legs and screaming into the pillows.

"Patience is a virtue," he finally says.

I feel wetness rushing from my warmest place staining the sheets. I'm breathing hard not knowing what to expect next. He touches my wetness, stirring it like soup. His feather-like touch drives me insane! He positions my legs into a doggie style position when I look back. He makes sure his sword is sheathed with a Trojan Fire and Ice condom before he positions himself behind me on his knees to plunge into my sloppy wetness.

"Juicy just like I like it," he says.

He thrusts slowly and is enjoying our union when something very strange happens. There is a tingling that resonates from his shaft

212

and spreads to my walls, warming my insides. I feel the sensation moving into my belly as he touches the wall of my cervix. He changes positions, standing over me froggy style, changing again. He swings his right leg over my body, still hitting it from the back but he is positioned on my side. Damn I need a camera! Nobody will ever believe this!

The sensation from the condom must have been effecting him too because he begins making noises. I feel an orgasm coming and I pull off the restraints. He doesn't notice because his back is to me now. My vagina contracts, causing him to look back at me because he recognizes the feeling. He begins bouncing with more ferocity, hammering my G with more intensity. We both explode sounding like Jane and Tarzan in the Amazon.

He pauses to catch his breath momentarily before jumping from the bed. He comes to the head of the bed, releasing my restraints. He stands me up, leading me to a chair with no arms, which seems to be very low to the ground. He is sitting down to change the condom when I notice that his erection is still as hard as steel. Whew! Here we go again.

His shaft is thick and throbbing. He notices me looking and he asks, "Is it enough for you?"

I say, "I am pleasantly filled, thank you."

"Come face me so I can see your pleasure," he says.

I giggle and straddle him on the chair. I'm glad the chair is short because I am half his height! I glide him into my wetness again, pushing our legs closed. I hold on to the back of the chair, taking my time with his manhood. He grabs my breasts, sucking and biting my nipples as the tip of his manhood fills my walls and expands. My thighs begin to burn and he turns my body around, opening his legs so that I can fit between them. I close my legs, holding on to his thighs. I work his manhood from the back. He swings and smacks the hell out of my butt cheek. I scream with pleasure and he laughs low and guttural.

"I could tell by the way you were watching me you wanted me to spank you," he says.

I look back with my "Rock" eyebrow and beg for more. He grabs my hips and begins thrusting like a thoroughbred. He stands up holding me by the hips and I wrap my legs around his waist. I brace myself on the bed as he continues to pound his manhood deeper and deeper into my being. I scream as my body cums and cums and cums again. We roar together again then collapse face first onto the bed from complete exhaustion and ecstasy. I'm laying face first in the pillows and he is lying on his back. He turns to look at me, caressing my back with his fingertips.

"So how did you enjoy the Fetish Party?" you say.

"If it ends like this every time, I need to become a sponsor," I say. We both laugh.

"So may I see you again?" you ask.

"Any day you like, baby," I say.

THE ULTIMATE ADDICTION

You are the ultimate addiction

I crave you….all of you!

Not just your thick manhood

Ramming squirting and cumming all over me

But your verbal ejaculations

Planting seeds of hope love and expectations

I long to feel your masculinity

Stroking my femininity

Invoking my Eve from the depths of Genesis

To rise and take my Queenship beside you My King

I feel my purpose in God leap every time you vocalize your life's lessons

That pushes you into your destiny

Never have I felt so connected

To one individual through faith

Without experiencing their physical being

I can only imagine the explosion of kinetic energy

That will shake the universe

LOOK AT LOVE THROUGH MY EYES

At the slightest touch of your hand

Oh! How I anticipate that touch!

That will ignite the fire I feel inside of me now

Until I am completely consumed by you

And I am instantaneously transformed into the Isis you see

My addiction for you grows daily

Fed by the intonation in your voice

 When you call my name

Your passion and thirst for the Most High God

Your compassion for humanity

And your unconditional love for your daughters

I have never known an emotion as strong as this

Where *I love you* is not adequate enough

to express the explosion of emotion I feel in my heart

This emotion I feel erodes rational thought

I've got to be crazy right?

But I fiend for you, I long for you, I need you

My ultimate addiction.

BY INVITATION ONLY

We have been dating for several months now. We have enjoyed guilty pleasures that neither one of us expected. My favorite day was the picnic in the park that you strategically planned.

We drove to the lake to the place called the Overlook. You spread before me a petite feast of Turkey, brie, baguettes, my favorite Kettle chips, fresh fruit, and fresh chef salads. You were meticulous about matching the blanket, silver and plates, and I noticed the care you took in packing everything.

As we dined and lazily enjoyed the day, a sudden summer storm surprised us. I rushed to put the picnic basket together, when you stopped me. I looked up bewildered and you flashed me a mischievous smile. You pulled me to my feet and we sprinted to the nearest crop of bushes, where the foliage is so tall that no one can see us. You kissed me with eagerness as the rain joined us in the wetness of the moment. I began pulling at your clothes

LOOK AT LOVE THROUGH MY EYES

I wore a sundress, as you requested. Lucky me! You slowly rolled up my layers and toyed with my juices. To your surprise, I was not wearing any panties. As if Mother Nature was prepared for our adventure. I noticed a small, metal bench nestled between the bushes. Our minds click at the same time and we raced like teenagers to the bench. You sat with your manhood exposed to the elements, stroking it into rock hard readiness; moreover, you grinned like a Cheshire cat. I gathered my dress around my waist and straddled you, looking deep into your eyes. You engulfed me with your arms wrapped around my back. We kissed again, melding into nature with our lovemaking, feeling what Adam and Eve must have felt in worship, surrounded by the majesty of Eden.

Rain interfused with our passion as you nuzzled my neck, whispering lustful sentiments in my ear. I transitioned giving you my back to kiss, sliding easily back into position. You caressed my shoulders, allowing me to be in control at the moment. I pushed your knees together and balanced my weight as I spread my legs wider for

better leverage.

Anticipating the ride, you entangled my damp hair into your

large fist, pulling my head back. "Ride that shit, beautiful!" you

yelled.

With the rain battering our bodies, I arched my back like a cat

and bounced on your dick until you roared like Tarzan.

I giggle at the memory, watching you watching television from

your perch at the other end of the couch. You notice and say, "Penny

for your thoughts?"

"The Lake."

"Yes, great day," you say, raising your "Rock" eyebrow.

I look back at you, admiringly and you turn off the TV. "I have

a question for you," I say.

"Every time you say that, adventure cometh."

"Yes my love," I respond, looking cynical.

You continue. "My friend at work told me about a place in the mountains that you can only attend by invitation. He says it is a place that is totally uninhibited."

"How uninhibited?" I ask, with both eyebrows raised.

"Anything goes. Voyeurism, exhibition, two, three or all   out orgy. We can get a room for later. We pay one price, food is included and we bring our own drinks."

"Very interesting. And how far do you expect to go?" I ask, "Are you sure you want to go to this place with me?"

"All I ask is that you experience this with me. We can watch them make love in a private room or wherever you wish. It will be something new for us and I think you're open minded enough to handle it."

I look at you speculatively. "Ok I'll do it," I say. "What do I wear?"

"After five attire. I'll put my tux in the cleaners."

You gallop to the bedroom and my eyes follow your movements. My mind is reeling, wondering what I've gotten myself into this time.

The week goes by quickly, mainly because of the anticipation of the adventurous weekend planned. On the day of the event I drive slowly toward the cleaners, pondering what I'll see. I leave the cleaners and meander to your house. As I open the door, I hear music playing in the living room. Our bags are placed at the door and you are patiently waiting for my arrival. When you notice my entrance, you stand and hand me a glass of wine. As I hand you your tuxedo, you smile saying, "Thank you for consenting. I'm extremely excited."

"Let's get dressed before I change my mind," I say.

We separate, you heading for the bedroom, me heading for the shower. You hum incessantly while you dress and I just shake my head. I dress slowly and carefully, making sure that every piece of my Aiden Mattox red batwing sleeves satin dress, makeup, and hair is in place. You're standing in the doorway of the bathroom in your Sean John   Black Strip tuxedo and a Social Premiere bow tie that matches my dress.

"You are so beautiful. I might have a fight on my hands tonight."

I smile and say, "You ain't sharing this good lovin' with nobody and you know it."

You chuckle good-heartedly and motion for me to hurry. "Gather your things and I'll be in the car."

You sprint down the stairs and I get my Crystal Fox fur cape and slip on my Christian Louboutin Metal Nodo heels. As I sashay down the stairs I see you holding the car door open for me with this capacious grin on your face. You escort me to the car and we are on our way.

LOOK AT LOVE THROUGH MY EYES

We drive for what seems like hours. You caress my hand as I look out of the window at the scenery. We travel on the freeway and exit close to the South Carolina line. After a short drive in a clearing, maple trees adorn a long winding paved driveway leading to an immaculate estate. As we approach the gated entrance, I see a beautiful fountain with cherubs squirting water into crystal blue water. It has a pedestal in a lotus bowl where the light emits an eerie shadow onto the stone faces. The exterior Palladian windows of the house give it a historical elegance. The glow from the candles inside reflects a golden hue on the glass drawing attention to the glass paneled doors at the entrance of the estate.

Valets open the door to the car and welcome us quickly before dashing away. You offer me your arm and you feel me shaking with excitement.

"You stay close to me and we'll explore together, my delicate flower," you say.

LOOK AT LOVE THROUGH MY EYES

I hold on to you more firmly as we mount the stairs. The Victorian doors open to energetic, club style music blaring from the Bose Free Space Audio System. Aldric and Babette, our gracious hosts, meet us with open arms. They direct our bags to our room and briefly tell us where everything is situated. They inform us that the environment was open and encourage us to enjoy ourselves. From where I am standing, I can tell that we are on the ground level.

To my right is The Club, where people are dancing and laughing. To my left is a grand dining area with a feast fit for kings. In front of us is a mahogany stained oak railing with balusters. You pull me toward The Club when Sean Paul's *Just Give Me the Light* booms in the speakers. I giggle, shimmying with my shoulders. We join the small crowd and dance for what seems like hours. We sit on an empty bench sweaty, enjoying the moment. When you go and retrieve some refreshments, I notice another room connected to The Club. Through the oak doors I see chiffon panels draping a canopy style bed surrounding what seems like sitting areas.   You return and

notice the direction in which I am distracted.

"Come on let's see," you say.

You take my hand and place your arm around my waist.

We saunter through the door and sit on a bench positioned

in the center of the room. The canopies are not draped around

the seats; they are covering queen size beds. In each bed is an

assortment of couples or threesomes clothed, partially clothed, or

nude. I sit in total amazement just watching each group. The first

couple is mixed, black female and white male. He has entered her

from behind and she has her knees against the sides of his thighs

with her back to him. She is holding on to his neck, sitting upright

facing the crowd. He has his hand on her clitoris, and they are

moving slowly. She notices us looking and she licks her lips.

My attention shifts to the next bed where I see sudden

movement. Three people, two females and one male, have contorted

themselves into an interesting oral position. The male is on the bed propped up on several pillows in a sitting position. One female is sitting on his face grinding on his tongue. While she is grinding, she is holding the bottom-half of the other woman with her legs on her shoulders. She is eating the woman on her shoulders out like it's an all-you-can-eat buffet, while the women she is holding is sucking the hell out of the man's dick! I squeeze my legs together feeling really stimulated! You glance at me and ask with a sly grin on your face, "You want me to rub that for you?"

I smile and kiss you responding, "Not yet love. Let's explore some more rooms."

There is a set of glass doors that lead to a wooded terrace. We giggle as we enter what turns out to be a glassed enclosed porch. The scenic beauty of the landscape surrounding the house is breathtaking. You stand behind me, gathering me into your arms as we marvel at God's handiwork. We get lost in the view before we notice soft moans resonating in the room. We both turn slowly to see a couple on the chaise, oblivious to our presence.

LOOK AT LOVE THROUGH MY EYES

She has on a fire engine red dress that is tailored to be shorter in the front. It billows onto the floor in lavish ruffles, conveniently covering her body and his. His pants are crumpled at his feet around his shoes. She is facing him riding his manhood like she stole something. Sweat glistens on her back and her carefully pinned bun begins to loosen. Her hair cascades in curly strands around her head. He has this sedated look on his face and his eyes are rolling back into his head. This low gravelly moan is coming from his throat.

"I think we should explore somewhere else," I say laughing, softly.

We exit through another door leading to the dining area. We fill our plates and sit at an available table close to the wall so we can watch the crowd. We laugh, talk, touch, and tease each other while enjoying the exquisite cuisine.

"It's time to go upstairs. Are you ready?" you ask.

"Ready as I'll ever be," I say.

We leave the dining area with our drinks in hand. I'm sure I'm going to need a few before this night is over. We walk hand-in-hand up the spiral staircase and the corridor begins to narrow. At the top of the stairs to the left are rows of doors leading to the private rooms, one of which we have rented for later. I smile at the possibilities. To the right   is a set of intricately carved oak doors. They are the length and width   of the adjacent wall. They are wide open and red light beams from the entrance. Intrigued, we walk slowly to the opening with our heads cocked to the side.

"The Matrix" as it is affectionately called, is a room akin to a scene from Sodom and Gomorrah. Red lights and candles maintain an ambiance of low sensual illumination. There is barely three feet of room to walk around a colossal bed that fills the room completely. At the entrance is a giant three foot martini glass full of an assortment of condoms. Along the walls are benches for voyeurs to watch all of the action. We sit on the bench so that we can see the bed and the door. As our eyes adjust to the lighting a sea of bodies move with

229

agility all over the bed. Faces of all colors, sizes, and skill

encompass the room.

One man samples the variety of pussies with his tongue until he

finds one that agrees with his palette and reacts accordingly. He

wraps his arms around the woman's thighs, pulling her directly over

his head. She screams in excitement--until another man puts his dick

in her mouth. Another couple, obviously husband and wife and new

to the group, meekly have sex on the corner of the bed doggie style.

The wife is making small panting noises. A tall blond Amazon

comes over and begins kissing the husband. She pulls him away

from his wife and lies down next to her. The Amazon grabs the

husbands head and smashes his face into her vagina and he begins to

suck, lick, and bite like it's nobody's business. The wife is distracted

and does not see the 6' 3" Mandingo positioning himself behind her.

His initial push into her body causes her to let out a shrill sound that

sends chills down my spine. He is gentle with her at first, but when

he senses her comfort, he badgers her with such intensity that the crowd begins to cheer him on! His ejaculation is so strong that his scream causes the chandelier to tremble.

I am gushin' after that one!

"Damn that was some good shit! You're a lucky bastard!" he says, stumbling backward trying to catch his balance.

Several women rush to his side, placing his body on the corner of the bed caressing and stroking him back into action. The husband jumps back onto his wife but she returns to the old, tired reaction. I don't blame her after fucking with Mandingo! Her husband looks sadly disappointed. This obese white guy waltzes by with his wife on his arm; both are naked. He sees us on the bench and heads in our direction.

"Hey buddy, you want some of this?" He spins his wife around, swatting her on the ass.

"Naw man I'm good. Just enjoying the view," you respond.

"First timers, huh?" he asks. "Okay, no problem but your woman looks like she is about to pop. Bet that's some good pussy. Enjoy."

He and his wife turn and jump into the mass of bodies.

"Where is our room?" I ask. You smile in expectation and lead me into the hallway. We stop in front of door 313. As you open the door, my line of sight is drawn to the South Coast king canopy bed stationed in the middle of the room. Candle light glows from golden leaf Venetian mini chandeliers strategically placed in every corner. An arched entryway leads to a quaint washroom equipped with a standalone shower and a tub for two. You stand back watching me absorb the room as you gently close the door. I touch the paneling on the bed, admiring the traditional colonial intricacy of the bed posts design. I try to fathom the age of such craftsmanship and I get lost in the romance of the atmosphere. The Winchester fireplace adds to the milieu, providing warmth and comfort. I notice you looking at me with a wide grin, slowly removing your tuxedo suit jacket.

"You knew I'd love this room didn't you?" I ask.

"You are a hopeless romantic," you reply.

You glide toward me, unbuttoning your tuxedo shirt, kissing me gently, pulling me close to your body. I feel your desire rising as I fumble with your belt and zipper. You halt my hands and turn me around so you can unzip my dress. Gradually, you lower the zipper and push my dress from my shoulders. To your surprise I am wearing a red Daisy Strapless Burlesque corset attached to garters with no panties.

"Oh my gawd!" you exclaim, covering your mouth with one hand and pumping your fist in the air with the other.

We laugh and laugh.

"Girl you are always full of surprises!"

"That's what you adore about me." I gleam proudly.

You pull me close again, kissing me amorously. I feel your pants fall to the floor as I pull at your shirt. I start to unfasten the corset and you say, "Woo keep that on!" I giggle and begin to stroke

your manhood. I guide you to the bed and playfully push you down.

I gently take you into my mouth and begin massaging your head and

shaft with my tongue. I get it sloppy wet, just like you like it. When

you are hard as a rock, glistening and standing erect, I motion for

you to move into the middle of the bed. I climb onto the bed with you

turning my body to ride backwards. I straddle your right leg,

squatting low enough to touch my clitoris with the head of your

manhood. I love the way that feels and judging from your reaction, so

do you.

I am extremely moist from watching all of the action around the

house. I can feel my essence beginning to ooze from my vulva. I

guide you into me easily as I sit with my back to you. I can feel my

clitoris rubbing on your thigh as I prop myself up with my arms on

either side of your legs. I begin with a slow grind feeling the head of

your penis touching my cervix. You caress my back, whispering sweet

words expressing your love. As comfort sets in, I move with more urgency because of the sensation of my clitoris rubbing against your thigh and you filling me completely. I can feel an orgasm stretching from my toe nails, creeping through my calves, knees, thighs, buttocks; cresting in my vagina until my entire body quivers involuntarily.

A low rasping moan crescendos from my throat, turning into a high pitched squeal as I release, drenching your leg. You chuckle and I look back at you over my shoulder. You transition, pushing me down onto my face. There is a matching South Coast bed bench at the foot of the bed. You give me a pillow and instruct me to put the top half of my body on the bench lying on my stomach, while my legs remain on the bed. I look back inquisitively then put the pillow on the bench under my belly and I lie down. You open my legs and kneel behind me doggie style with my bottom elevated. You place my legs under you arms holding my knees.

You gently enter me from behind, knowing how deep you will get in this position. You grind into my inner most being until I lose my   breath. You swivel your hips until my reaction tells you that you have found my G-Spot. Your motions become purposeful. You painstakingly focus your attention on my pleasure. My legs begin to quake again and the endorphins in my head tingle from the rush of blood to my brain. I pull at my hair, not knowing if I should scream or pull away. With every thrust of your thickness, I cum and cum and cum. You grunt every time my orifice contracts with every orgasm tightening around your shaft. You press in enjoying the sensation as I raise my "church" finger in surrender. You sigh, pulling out and helping me back onto the bed.

"You've been reading again," I say after collecting myself.

"Yep!" you say, as you stroke your manhood in your hand.

"So have I, so let's try something strange. Do you remember the lyrics from Prince's *Insatiable*? I want your hips in the air."

You lay on your back with this astonished look on your face. I instruct you to hug your knees with your legs open. Your eyes get as big as a deer in headlights and I laugh. You consent and I position myself above you froggie style over your legs. I insert your penis into my vagina and balance myself with my hands on your thighs. I bounce slowly watching your expression.

"I feel like a bitch!" you exclaim.

"My bitch, baby," I say with a wink

When my thighs begin to burn, I put my knees down leaning in closer to your body in a kneeling Amazon position. I bob on your dick as you close your eyes enjoying my work. I increase my thrusts and you reach for the sheets, holding on for dear life. As I bear down I can feel your manhood throbbing, indication your release is near. I reposition my hands for better stability and I ride as if my life depends on it. You close your eyes even tighter, gasping for air. Then you release a roar that could awaken the dead. I cum with you feeling our essence intermingle and run freely from my body. Your toes are curled and teasingly tickle my feet. I roll onto the bed sweaty, sated and smiling.

LOOK AT LOVE THROUGH MY EYES

You put your legs down and sigh heavily. "Don't you go telling nobody you did that to me."

I laugh heartily, swearing to secrecy. We lay there for a moment basking in the afterglow. You lean on one arm facing me, freeing me of the corset and garters. We talk, laugh, touch, enjoying each other's company. We make love again until we pass out from exhaustion.

In the morning we shower, dress, pack and head downstairs for breakfast. The Matrix doors are closed and we hear jazz playing in the Club. The breakfast buffet is just as massive as dinner was the previous night. We recognize faces from various parts of the house and we nod in acknowledgement. Our gracious hosts reappear, chatting with all of the guests. We have small talk as we finish our food. Before leaving we go to the patio once more to admire the view of the landscape. We walk through the house, remembering all that we saw.

As we reach the patio, you gather me into your arms again.
I get lost in your warmth when you say, "Thank you for coming here
with me."

I turn to face you, touching your cheek. "You weren't coming
here without me."

We genuinely laugh. We turn to leave as the concierge is
bringing our bags down from the room. Aldric and Babette bid us
ado until next time. Then the car arrives from valet. We drive quietly
home and I can't help but wonder what our next adventure will be.

ABOUT THE AUTHOR

Loquacious Even has been teaching special education for 14 years in North Carolina. Outside of the classroom, she teaches adolescents' social and table etiquette, and positive self-image promotion. By night, she specializes in teaching adults sexual self-awareness for their fulfillment in relationships. She has also worked as a Pure Romance consultant for several years.

Please go to
Facebook.com/lookatlovethroughmyeyes
and LIKE the fan page!

Check out the commercial on
youtube.com/loquaciouseven

241

Made in the USA
Columbia, SC
25 February 2022

56834894R00137